About

Martin McKenna is the author of the best-selling *The Dog Man* and *What's Your Dog Telling You?* He learned about dog behaviour in a very unusual way: as a boy growing up in Limerick, Ireland, he escaped from family violence by running away from home and living in a barn with a pack of stray dogs. By observing these street dogs at such close quarters, he learned the unique psychology and language shared by dogs all over the world. Now he's passionate about helping dogs and humans communicate more successfully with each other.

To Teresa,

Amazing "what dogs can teach you"! No doubt Chica & Logan will give you even more happiness after reading This book.

Best Wishes & love, Brigitte xx.

WHAT'S YOUR DOG TEACHING YOU ?

WHAT'S YOUR DOG TEACHING YOU?

Martin McKenna

ABC
Books

The ABC 'Wave' device is a trademark of the
Australian Broadcasting Corporation and is used
under licence by HarperCollins*Publishers* Australia.

First published in Australia in 2013
by HarperCollins*Publishers* Australia Pty Limited
ABN 36 009 913 517
harpercollins.com.au

HarperCollins*Publishers*
Level 13, 201 Elizabeth Street, Sydney NSW 2000, Australia
31 View Road, Glenfield, Auckland 0627, New Zealand
A 53, Sector 57, Noida, UP, India
77–85 Fulham Palace Road, London W6 8JB, United Kingdom
2 Bloor Street East, 20th floor, Toronto, Ontario M4W 1A8, Canada
10 East 53rd Street, New York NY 10022, USA

National Library of Australia Cataloguing-in-Publication data:

McKenna, Martin.
    What's your dog teaching you? / Martin McKenna.
    ISBN: 978 0 7333 3167 1 (pbk.)
    Human–animal relationships.
    Dogs — Behavior.
    Dogs — Psychology.
636.70835

Original cover design by Design by Committee,
    adapted by HarperCollins Design Studio
Cover images: Dachshund looking up by Gandee Vasan/Getty Images;
    all other images by shutterstock.com
Typeset in Sabon 10.5/15pt by Kirby Jones
Printed and bound in Australia by Griffin Press
The papers used by HarperCollins in the manufacture of this book are a natural,
recyclable product made from wood grown in sustainable plantation forests. The fibre
source and manufacturing processes meet recognised international environmental
standards, and carry certification.

5 4 3 2 1   13 14 15 16

To the incredible family I love:
Lee, Siggy, Casey, Fintan and Marie;
to the most supportive brothers in the world:
Andrew and John;
to my darling angel of a mother, Sigrid, now gone;
and all the unforgettable dogs I've met — each one of you has
profoundly changed my life for the better, so thank you.

Contents

Introduction

What valuable lessons can dogs teach us about life?

Dogs have taught me so much.

As a miserable, angry, mixed-up street kid in Garryowen, Ireland, I hated the world, but when I hooked up with a pack of the local stray dogs I suddenly found I had a family again — even if it was a rather unusual, hairy one. Feeling safe and secure, I could finally put away the nightmare memories of alcohol and violence and bullying.

This pack of strays lived with me in an old hay barn for just over three years but it didn't take me long to realise that these street dogs were becoming my teachers in all sorts of ways.

They taught me the meaning of courage and responsibility and staunch loyalty. They taught me to give and get affection again. They taught me that I could trust others again and, more importantly, they showed me how to cautiously work out who I could trust. They brought out my curiosity and got me thinking laterally and showed me how to solve problems creatively. They taught me to care for someone other than myself. They taught me how to stand up to bullies. They gave me back my sense of self-worth. They taught me how to have a truly optimistic attitude.

Best of all, they taught me how to become a much better communicator.

This was so important because if you can't communicate properly with anyone else you soon find yourself locked in an invisible cage of profound loneliness. As I learned to communicate better — first with these street dogs, then with people — I began to hesitantly find my place in the world of humans again.

From being a skinny, lonely freak of a kid, I believe dogs helped me to grow up into the gregarious, calm, loving, optimistic man I am today. Sometimes I look back and can't believe what a long, rocky road I've travelled. Just as amazingly over the years, I've seen dogs profoundly transform the lives of many other people too. After all, who knows us better than our dog? They live with us in our homes — sometimes sharing the couch and even the bed.

Their powers of observation are remarkable. Just think of how many hours this natural-born predator spends carefully watching us, studying every one of our movements, postures, gestures and facial expressions, trying to work out what we'll do next. Designed to be a pack animal that's highly sensitive to the politics within a small group, dogs are superbly aware of the shifting dynamics between every member of our household. Even more amazingly, dogs can *smell* exactly how we're feeling, so we can't even get away with faking our emotions around our dog.

Yes, our dog knows us almost frighteningly well: all our foibles, our moods, our strengths and our weaknesses, what triggers us to lose our temper, and what calms us down when we're upset. You could say our dog knows us inside out.

I believe a dog could be one of the most influential teachers a person can ever have. In this book are the true stories of dogs I've known who've acted as profound teachers for their human owners. Sixty valuable life-lessons that dogs can teach us — if only we're willing to listen.

1

What can dogs teach us about ourselves?

Nobody knows you as well as your dog. It lives with you and watches every single one of your gestures and postures, knows all your facial expressions, and recognises by the sound of your footsteps exactly what sort of mood you're in. Even more incredibly, your dog can smell your true feelings. That's why it walks cautiously up behind you and delicately sniffs at the air. If you're feeling anxious or angry, sad or frustrated, and you're trying to fake that you're happy — well, forget it. Your dog has the most intimate knowledge of how you *really* feel.

Since our dog knows us so well, let's see what it can teach us about ourselves.

You become what you believe

As a kid, I believed I was worth nothing.

I couldn't make my family love me. I couldn't make friends. I couldn't learn anything at school. I couldn't read.

I couldn't write. I couldn't communicate with people. These were all the things that I believed about myself.

Then dogs started to transform how I thought about myself. They stopped me believing that insidious voice inside my head that said such negative things.

No one wants to listen to anything you have to say, Martin.

As a mixed-up, angry street kid, I kept all my fears, anger and problems bottled up inside. Then I moved into an old hay barn with a pack of Garryowen strays. By the end of three years, those dogs taught me to communicate in a much better way with everyone around me — whether they were dog or human. These days I've changed so much I now actually teach other people how to communicate better — especially with their dogs.

You'll never achieve anything, Martin — you've always been useless.

However, each small breakthrough I achieved with dogs made me realise that I was far from useless, that I was in fact capable of achieving whatever I wanted if I worked my butt off. Each dog language signal I managed to translate for the first time, each dog I was able to save, each behaviour program I worked out for difficult dogs — all of these breakthroughs really changed how I thought about myself.

Why? Each discovery I had with dogs gave me the confidence to tackle the other challenges in my life. For example, I was terrified of being a father but I've ended up being a surprisingly great dad to my four wonderful kids. I finally learned how to be a great husband. I got a mortgage and a small farm for my family. This is my third book. I learned how to promote my books well — being on hundreds of radio shows, as well as TV — and bring my message to a wider audience. Recently, I've pitched my innovative art work to some of the best art dealers in the country and it's beginning to stir interest in the right circles.

You'll never be able to read and write, Martin — you're far too stupid.

Funnily enough, learning to read and write has been one of the scariest challenges I've ever had to face, after my nightmare school experiences — just *thinking* of reading and writing would make me break into a cold sweat. However, when my youngest daughter, Marie, was reading and writing like a pro in primary school I decided it was ridiculous to feel so terrified of something that my seven-year-old found easy and fun. So I decided to finally bite the bullet and learn how to read and write.

My wife, Lee, a natural-born teacher, was tough and blunt with me. She knew me well enough to understand I didn't want to learn by using baby books. Instead, she gave me a task that she knew would drive me to succeed.

'Start writing down all those poems of yours,' she said. 'I believe you'll be able to read and write something if you keep doing that.'

Well, I sure fought that idea.

Then she stopped writing my poems down for me and I had no choice but to try. She showed no mercy. 'Plunge straight in. Write those poems of yours down in an exercise book and keep on scribbling them down.'

She wrote the alphabet down for me on the inside cover of every exercise book. I was painfully slow to start with, my spelling was atrocious, and a lot of my writing couldn't even be read it was so messy.

I'd get so frustrated and ask Lee to help me write down a good poetry line before I forgot it, but she was implacable. 'You're writing it down, not me.' She wouldn't fuss, she'd just hand me endless packets of pens and exercise books and say, 'Don't worry, eventually all that scribble is going to be transformed into something readable.'

Some very frustrating months went by. Sometimes I'd look at the pen in my hand and want to rip it apart with my teeth because it wouldn't do what I wanted it to. Then I'd look down at the dog at my side and say to myself, 'Well, at least my writing's better than yours, dog.'

So that's how I learned to write a few years ago. Hard as it is to believe, I then learned to read by simply re-reading all those thousands and thousands of poems I'd scribbled down in exercises books out on my verandah.

Funnily enough, even as a kid I never believed I was a coward. But again dogs have been the reason I've always thought I've had plenty of courage. Here's my secret way of rallying together every scrap of my courage when I'm in a crisis situation, whether that's standing outside a meeting room, preparing to give a big project pitch, or simply facing a big, mean bugger of a dog who wants to rip my leg off. When I need lots of courage this is what I do. I visualise the bravest, most daring dog I can think of and I pretend to act like it. I breathe like the dog, walk like it, hold myself like it and even *think* in some ways like that dog. Then in my mind, as I walk into the crisis, I just keep calmly and silently repeating this word to myself: Staunch!

Over the years I've borrowed the courage of so many brave, daring, even audacious dogs I've known — Paddyboy, Jack, Fianna, Pip, Sean — and many others. Crazy, isn't it? But strangely enough, this simple visualisation technique has brought me fantastic results over the years.

Maybe you can try using it yourself. If you're ever having trouble believing in yourself, just borrow the courage of a gutsy, daring dog you've known. Visualise that you're inside the skin of that dog and silently repeat to yourself: Staunch! Now nothing nor no one is going to be able to scare you. If you can't believe in yourself, borrow the required courage from dogs and plunge straight into that next challenge without fear or hesitation.

Live a more adventurous life

Feeling a little stale and bored lately? Try adding more adventure to your life.

Neville desperately wanted to spice up his life. He was sixty-two and asked me to come and help him with his Pekingese called Hugo.

On my arrival, Hugo turned his little squashed-in nose and dark button eyes to give me a regal look. Then, jumping up onto the couch next to Neville, he turned his back and dismissed me instantly.

'Here's my problem,' Neville said, 'over the years, Hugo and I have become stuck in a rut'. He fondly stroked Hugo's immense apricot-coloured mane. 'I've had him for seven years and unfortunately we've become two boring bachelors living together. I want to start going out evenings so I can mix with people, however, Hugo starts to panic if I leave him on his own. The poor fellow isn't used to it.'

I smiled — Neville and Hugo did look like two settled bachelors sitting comfortably next to each other on the couch.

'We can fix that,' I said easily.

I took Neville through a program where he could leave Hugo home alone without having the dog barking and howling down the house. Before I drove away an hour later, I promised to return the following week to see how things were progressing.

On my next visit, however, Neville looked rather nervous as he ushered me inside and sat me down. Hugo disdainfully gave me his superior look, then turned his back on me, pretending I didn't exist.

I wondered if Neville had been having second thoughts about my behaviour program. 'Everything all right?'

'Oh yes — your program's working like a dream.' He sat up straighter and looked me in the eye. 'However, I need your advice about women.'

I felt my eyebrows rise. *Women?* This was a first from a dog client. 'Okay — shoot.'

'In the last fortnight I've been out several times — to a few social clubs.'

'Excellent,' I said.

'But I didn't enjoy myself. Unfortunately, the ladies were rather difficult to talk to. I was wondering if —' He took a bracing breath. 'If you might advise me about where I could go to spend some *quality* time with ladies.' He looked absolutely red-faced with embarrassment as though he'd asked the most delicate question in the world.

I looked at Neville blankly — then felt myself blush for the first time in years. Was he asking my advice on bordellos? Strip clubs? Dating agencies? I gazed at him in confusion.

Neville squirmed in his chair and stared down at his hands, blushing even more than me. 'I have to admit I've always had a secret hankering to spend time with the ladies … um … dancing — ballroom dancing.'

Somehow, I stopped myself from laughing out loud in relief. Funnily enough, I could just picture Neville sweeping a beautifully gowned lady around a ballroom floor.

'The trouble is, I've always been *terrified* of asking the ladies to dance. I'm hopeless — two left feet, you know. But I thought you might have some ideas of how I might go about starting.'

I thought for a moment. 'Why not sign up for a dancing class? I bet they'll love having an extra man join up.'

'Oh dear — that sounds scary,' he said.

'What's the alternative?' I pointed out. 'Say you don't sign up for the dancing classes. In three years' time, do you know what? Nothing will have changed — and you and Hugo will *still* be sitting here on this couch, watching TV every single night till one of you dies first.'

Neville laughed nervously. 'Not a very inspiring thought is it?'

'You know what they say — Who dares wins.'

A bold glint flared briefly in his eyes. He patted Hugo with a far more vigorous stroke than usual. 'Sorry old fellow, but you'll have to stay home alone a bit more because I'm off to go dancing with the ladies.' He turned to me. 'Looks like there's still a bit of life left in *this* old dog after all.'

Hugo looked out from under his long mane at us suspiciously.

I ran into Neville a few years later and he was looking very dapper, with an amazing new aura of confidence around him. There was now a certain extra dashing, debonair air about him.

'How's Hugo?' I asked after we warmly shook hands. 'Did the behaviour program work okay?'

'Hugo's flourishing, thank you. Your program worked wonderfully.'

'And the dancing classes were a success?'

He smiled proudly. 'You won't believe it, but I'm quite a splendid dancer.'

'And any special lady you prefer as your dancing partner?'

He gave me a slow, cheeky wink. 'Oh, I'm afraid these days I prefer to have a *choice* of ladies to dance with,' he said. 'I must thank you, if I hadn't taken up dancing classes I'm afraid I'd *still* be watching TV with Hugo every night.'

We shook hands and he walked away, an unmistakable lift in his step. I watched him, imagining how he must cause many a lady's heart to flutter and a flirtatious smile to curve her lips as he swept her smoothly around the dance floor.

I briefly wondered what Hugo thought of the more adventurous Neville. Surely he preferred his master's wonderful new liveliness. Dogs are naturally drawn to the exciting energy of adventurous people — but then again, aren't we all?

Are you stuck in a rut? Try adding more risk to your life. No need to trek up the Amazon River, simply take some new classes, get out of your comfort zone, play around with your scariest fears. Nothing gets the energy pumping inside you like living a more adventurous life.

Stop worrying about what everyone else thinks of you

Do you worry too much about what other people think about you? Hannah's little dog taught her to worry more about what she thought of herself.

I met Hannah down at a dog exercise park. She was having problems with her Maltese-cross-Poodle, Dominic. He was a dominant little personality and had taken to mounting people's legs in public, wrapping his paws around their calves, then rubbing himself in an excited frenzy against their shins. It was his way of dominating people and leaving his scent all over them.

One day I happened to be at the park and saw Dominic in frenzied action, wrapped around a horrified man's leg. Hannah was thoroughly embarrassed by Dominic's behaviour and rushed over to the rescue the poor man.

'Oh, I'm so sorry!' she said, almost in tears as she pulled Dominic off the man's leg. 'I truly am so sorry! Oh dear, what must you think of me?'

She clipped Dominic on his leash and dragged him away, her face crimson with embarrassment as she murmured under her breath, 'Oh my goodness — what must that man think of me? How embarrassing! How am I going to show my face around here again? Oh, I can't believe this. What must everyone in the park be thinking of me?' All the while she held her head down in shame and didn't dare look at anyone. Meanwhile, bold little Dominic wasn't giving a damn what anyone else thought of him. He'd scored big points for getting away with dominating a stranger and he was feeling mighty cocky and proud of himself.

I glanced around — aside from a few curious stares and some good-natured laughter, the people in the park weren't thinking about Hannah much at all. They were just looking at Dominic, perhaps thinking, 'What a bold little bugger of a dog, he looks a right handful. Glad I don't have to try to keep him under control.'

In my usual fashion, I fell into step with Hannah, explaining who I was and suggesting how we could introduce a program to change Dominic's behaviour if she was interested.

After thanking me and agreeing to try my ideas, Hannah repeated that same curious sentence I'd overheard earlier, 'Oh dear, what must you think of me?'

I glanced across at her but it was obvious she wasn't aware of how often she said the sentence. I was to soon learn that it wasn't just Dominic's rude behaviour that kept causing this sentence to pop out of Hannah's mouth. Almost anything that happened to her would cause her to drop her head in shame and murmur, 'Oh dear, what must everyone think of me?'

For instance, when we reached her home, she said, 'Oh dear, the house is such a mess —'

I guessed what was coming next.

'— what must you think of me?'

We sat down on the seats on her verandah and I started suggesting some changes that she could introduce into

Dominic's life so he didn't feel nearly so dominant. An hour later, she realised she hadn't offered me anything to drink and it was the same refrain: 'Oh how terribly rude I must seem. What must you think of me?'

We kept talking but that same sentence kept popping up. It got to the point that I had to say something.

'Hannah,' I said. 'We have to prove to little Dominic here that you're a worthy leader. But you're not giving him the right message, darling. If you're the boss, you can't worry any more about what everyone else thinks of you, because it's actually a very submissive way to think.'

'What do you mean?'

'Each time you ask, "What must you think of me?" you're actually making some sort of negative judgement about yourself. For example, "How weird I am because my dog mounts someone's leg." Or, "How silly I am for not controlling my dog better." "How dirty I am if my house is a little untidy at the moment." Or, "How rude I am not to have offered you a drink."

'Can you hear how many negative things you say to yourself every day when you ask that horrible question?'

'That's one hell of a lot of negative things, isn't it?'

I gestured at Dominic, who was strutting happily around the garden. 'Be like that dog of yours. He might get things wrong every now and again — but look how confident he is. He certainly doesn't waste any energy worrying what everyone else thinks of him.' I took her hand. 'Promise me you'll never say that sentence ever again.'

She hesitated, then shook my hand with surprising firmness. 'I promise. Never again.'

It's true — once you're comfortable in your own skin, you're not going to give a damn what anyone else thinks of you, you're only going to care about what you think of yourself. And I think that's when you finally start focusing on transforming yourself into someone you really like and admire.

Why don't you try it? Erase the sentence, 'Oh dear, what must people think of me?' from your life. It's a sentence not worthy of you.

Stop being a 'yes' person

You can't always be agreeable and fall in with what everyone else wants, otherwise you're going to find you're constantly lying to someone — usually yourself. If you secretly suspect you're a natural-born yes person — and you want to change — start asking yourself why you keep on agreeing with everyone around you, even if deep down you often want to say no.

Are you afraid if you stop going along with someone else's plans — they won't like you? Are you desperately trying to gain someone's approval? Be more exciting? Are you worried about hurting someone's feelings? Are you just too lazy to argue your own point of view? Are you afraid of someone's reaction if you say no? Are you worried you won't have any friends if you don't automatically fall in with their plans?

Really try to be honest with yourself the next time you have to say yes or no to someone. For once, really listen to your gut feeling. If your gut says no then make that word come out of your mouth. Even if you're scared — just say it anyway and see what happens.

Still too scared to say no?

Try this experiment with your dog the next time it's in a very demanding mood: keep on saying yes to your dog. No matter what your dog demands of you — you're going to agree and just go along with it. The word no isn't going to pass your lips. So if your dog constantly wanders over and demands that you pat it — just say yes every single time and pat it. If it jumps up on you, just say yes and let it jump all over you. If it demands that you feed it, just say yes and keep feeding it. If it wants to bark non-stop, just say yes and let it keep barking non-stop.

As things get more hectic — look around you. Is your dog nipping you excitedly because you're being such a weak target? Is it jumping all over you? Is it giving you a headache with all its barking? How do you feel inside? Is your gut twisting miserably inside because you feel so damned uncomfortable about everything?

Basically, if you keep on saying yes all the time to everyone in your life then you'll end up with a miserable twisting feeling in your gut all the time.

Being honest with yourself is the most effective formula there is for happiness and success. So the next time you want to say no to someone, don't make a big deal of it. Stay calm and relaxed and let it fall naturally from your lips. No matter what reaction you get from other people — just listen to your gut feeling. Sometimes you just have to do your own thing in your own way, no matter what anyone else thinks or says of you.

Don't waste any more time dwelling in the past — start living in the now

The one thing that I love about dogs is the way they don't dwell on the past like we tend to. Dogs have brains that are wired to live in the now, in other words, in the moment, because their wild ancestors had to be permanently switched on high alert in order to survive. We humans have a different brain design that allows our mind to constantly roam in all sorts of directions — into the past and future as well as the present moment.

The trouble with human thinking is that it can get stuck in a groove that stops us from realising how happy we could be right now. Sometimes we waste so much time dreaming or worrying about our future — or dwelling on our past — that we forget to enjoy ourselves right now.

Mark's dog taught him it wasn't worth dwelling on his past any longer.

I was called out to see Mark's dog, Blue, because it was knocking over Olivia, his two-year-old daughter, every chance it got. Mark's fiancée, Tess, was demanding that he do something about it.

'Mark's treating his dog as though it's far more important than his daughter,' Tess confided angrily, as she let me through the gate to their backyard. 'Watch this.'

Straightaway, I saw Blue bump Olivia to the ground at least six times — getting stronger with each bump so she really went flying. I looked at Mark, but it was obvious he wasn't really taking it in. It was almost as though Olivia was invisible.

I took a deep breath. No wonder Tess was so furious with him.

'You should be protecting your daughter better,' I said. 'Don't you love her?'

Mark looked at me in astonishment. 'Of course, I love Olivia — she's my daughter, for God's sakes.'

'Then why is she flat out on the ground with her face planted in the dirt?' I asked. 'Since I've arrived you haven't lifted a finger to stop Blue from knocking her over. Why's that?'

'Blue's a good dog. He just gets a bit excited, that's all.'

'He's hurting her,' I said. 'It's time to wake up — Blue needs to learn some manners. He also needs to know that you care much more about Olivia than him. Basically, nothing's going to change until you make Tess and Olivia the most important things in your life.'

His head dropped to a sulky, stubborn angle — an angle I've come to recognise in many of my male clients over the years. I'd learned how to deal with this particular attitude: be as direct as possible.

'Okay, spit it out — why is this dog the only thing you trust?' I demanded. 'Come on, let's hear it. There's obviously some big issue lurking around in your past, and for the sake of Olivia, it's time you deal with it.'

Mark glared at me furiously. Then his shoulders sank and he folded his arms tight. 'Okay ... okay ... you obviously know what you're talking about,' he muttered. 'The truth is my dad ran away from my mum and I when I was eleven years old. One day he was there — the next he was gone.' He took a deep breath. 'I'm always scared the people closest to me are going to walk away and abandon me without warning one day.'

Tess walked over and hugged him tightly. 'Mark, why didn't you tell me?'

He smiled shakily. 'Too ashamed, I guess.' He nodded over at his dog. 'I suppose every time Blue wanted me to pat him, it just made me feel loved. And I've always loved the way Blue followed me around everywhere, because it meant, well, he wasn't running away from me, was he?'

I showed them the new respectful manners I wanted Blue to learn.

'But of course, Mark, the main thing you've got to show your dog is how important your daughter is to you. That means you've got to stop dwelling on the past and enjoy living right now, with Tess and Olivia.'

It was time to go. I was glad to see Mark carrying Olivia in his arms as he walked me back to my car.

'Hell, Martin, asking you for help with a dog is like going to boot camp for emotions,' he said, shaking his head wryly. 'Thanks for dragging me out of my past today. I feel lighter already.'

'No problem,' I said and meant it.

If you're like Mark then I urge you to stop wasting any more time rehashing the past. I had to learn this tough lesson myself. Change your way of thinking and start living in the here and now because otherwise, you're only being the weakest possible version of yourself. If you need help learning how to live in the present moment just watch your dog in action throughout the day. To your dog, everything's happening right now. He isn't feeling any emotion other than what he needs to feel at this exact moment in time.

When you start living in the present, you'll stop dragging around all those old, sad, frightened emotions that you felt during the worst times in your life. So throw off your past! Believe me, it'll be like removing a massive load from your shoulders because, as you're no doubt aware by now, painful emotions are very heavy things to carry around indeed.

Learn to fill your personal space

When it comes to your personal space fill it proudly and confidently, otherwise bullies will be tempted to see how far they can push you.

Liz had an incredibly weak sense of personal space. Not only was she being bullied by most of her colleagues at work, she was also being bullied by her feisty Yorkshire terrier, Stanley.

When Liz sat me down and told me her problem of being bullied by Stanley, I grinned. 'Don't worry, I'm going to get you filling your personal space proudly. Then no one — not even Stanley — is going to be able to bully you again.'

She looked at me, then her eyes dropped to her lap. Stunned, I saw a single tear roll down her cheek. I reached across and touched her hand gently.

'That tear was sitting pretty close to the surface — what's wrong? Is there someone else bullying you besides Stanley?'

Liz looked up at me and tried to form a smile on her lips. 'Yes — at work. It's pretty horrible actually.' She flicked me an embarrassed glance. 'My work colleagues have been teasing me about my weight. They pretend it's only light-hearted joking, but it's not. Of course, then I come home and just gorge myself in front of the TV all night.'

She nodded at Stanley. 'I got a little dog to keep me company and make me feel loved — but he just bullies me too. Yesterday he nipped me because I was a bit slower than usual feeding him so I decided I'd had enough and called you.'

I hugged her hard. 'Well, I'm glad you called. Believe me, by the time we're finished here today you won't be letting anyone ever bully you again — not Stanley and not anyone at your office either.'

She laughed a bit tearfully.

'Come on — let's get started straightaway.' I held out my hand for Stanley's leash and she handed it to me. 'Liz, you have this wonderful big female body like a Rueben's masterpiece, but you have such an incredibly weak sense of personal space. Watch how easily I can push you around without even touching you.'

I started walking towards her with Stanley and, as I knew she would, she melted away.

She giggled nervously. 'What are you doing?'

I walked towards her some more. She stepped back instantly. I blocked and turned her until she was trying her hardest to flatten herself against the wall.

'See that?' I said. 'You just keep handing everyone else your personal space without putting up any sort of a fight.' I nodded down at Stanley. 'Even this little squirt is finding it easy to push you around.'

I held out my hand and led her back to the middle of the living room.

'Now,' I said. 'I want to start feeling your voice, your body and your energy completely fill your entire personal space.' I used my hands to show her the invisible bubble she needed to start imagining around herself. 'At the moment, Liz, you're so ashamed about your weight that you're desperately trying to squeeze yourself into just a tiny corner of this bubble.' I made my voice gentle. 'Worse — if anyone else moves towards you with their own bubble, you don't think yours is important enough to stand on that bit of ground and you just melt submissively out of their way. No wonder all the bullies at work — and even Stanley here — are at you all the time. You're such a tempting target for them.'

I gave her a few pointers on how to start filling her personal space bubble more confidently. I explained how everything that came out of her mouth didn't sound confident — that it came out as an apology or a question as though she was asking for permission. She hardly made any statements — and gave no commands at all. Neither did she hold up her chin to look people confidently in the eye: her chin was often tilted down as though in shame or embarrassment — a permanently submissive position. As Liz walked around, she didn't fill her personal space in a confident way. If anyone moved even slightly in her direction, she automatically stepped backwards with an apology.

Her energy also felt very weak. I got her really working on her breathing — filling up her lungs deeply and confidently instead of light, shallow breathing.

She chuckled. 'Breathing so deeply like this feels like I'm really pumping myself up — it feels great!'

We went for another walk around the house and garden with Stanley but this time it was a completely different woman on the end of the leash. This new Liz walked taller. She walked confidently, right in the centre of her space. She stopped taking submissive steps to give way to her dog. If he stopped and tried to block her she walked straight through him calmly.

At the end of several circuits of the house, I called a halt because Liz now filled her personal space perfectly. Even I was stunned at how different she was. Instead of the shy, overweight lady who'd opened the door to me, I now stood before a regal goddess. I thought she was going to cry a bit but she shocked me by laughing and flinging her arms around me happily.

'It's like you've unlocked me from being stuck inside this horrible cage. I felt so vulnerable before but now I feel free.'

She did cry eventually, with tears of pride and happiness when she rang me at the end of the week to tell me she was no longer getting bullied at work. I walked on air for weeks.

If you suspect you're not filling your personal space as well as you might be, clip your dog on a leash and practise taking back the space that's rightfully yours. Don't mistake good manners for lack of confidence. Don't offer a tempting target to bullies. You deserve to shine, so go ahead and proudly fill your personal space with confidence and vitality.

Learn how to control your own energy

I used to have a big problem not being able to manage my energy properly. I have ADHD — Attention Deficit

Hyperactivity Disorder — and the only way I can describe it is to say it's like drinking a thousand glasses of Coca-Cola. Over the years I've worked hard at learning to harness my ADHD energy so it doesn't keep exploding out of me in all directions. It's always interesting to see how far I've progressed when I go to see a client about their dog and someone in the household has ADHD.

One such household I visited belonged to Margo and Dean, a husband and wife who had a Staffy-cross called Charlie. This dog was driving the neighbours crazy because he'd sometimes erupt into noisy barking as he raced around the yard.

When I arrived, Margo and Dean were waiting for me in their front yard. Their son, James, was desperately trying to call Charlie, but the dog was just racing manically around the yard faster and faster. Dean was in his early forties and I picked him as a fellow suffer with ADHD the moment I saw him.

Even though he was standing still and silent, Dean was emanating ferocious amounts of energy. His dog Charlie was reacting to it by going crazy: rushing around the yard, almost somersaulting as he bounced off the high wooden paling fence before racing manically in another direction. Dogs, like most animals, are very sensitive to energy. They're actually like a sponge in the way they can't help but absorb all the energy coming off humans. However, the trouble is if energy gets absorbed into the dog then the dog at some point has to rid itself of all that excess energy.

In Dean's case, he was pumping out frustrated, barely suppressed hyperactive energy and his dog, Charlie, couldn't help but absorb it. In a desperate attempt to get rid of it from his system, the poor dog was trying to exercise it out before he suffocated.

Meanwhile, I could see Margo and James eyeing each other nervously. They were clearly sensing Dean was heading for an ADHD explosion where anything could happen. He was like a pressure cooker about to explode.

I took in a deep, calming breath. 'Okay, everyone, we're all going to relax and do something about this crazy energy around us before it gets completely out of control.'

They were stunned that I understood their family situation so well.

'The first thing we're going to do,' I said, 'is help calm down this poor dog.'

I demonstrated for them the natural dog calming signals that dogs use among themselves and soon we were all sitting down, acting lazy and sleepy, yawning and ignoring the dog. Charlie almost immediately went and laid down in the corner.

'Wow!' said James. 'That's so cool.'

'Now, Dean,' I said. 'I know how hard it is to get a grip on this ADHD of yours, but ultimately you're going to have to take responsibility for controlling your own energy. It not only affects you, it affects everyone around you. As we just saw, you're shredding your family's nerves apart — even your dog's.'

I gestured at his wife and son. 'It's not just Charlie who's feeling overwhelmed by all that explosive energy of yours — everyone sitting around this table is affected by it every day. Being around you is like being flattened by an invisible steamroller, isn't it, Margo and James?'

They laughed and agreed.

We discussed how Dean could better control his energy. Exercise, walks, playing his guitar, eating well — all kinds of ideas were mentioned.

Dean shook his head in amazement. 'I can't believe you have ADHD too, Martin. You're so bloody relaxed.'

'This is how you'll be — once you learn to control your energy.'

'I just can't imagine ever getting a handle on this energy of mine,' admitted Dean. 'It just zooms out of control so quickly — sometimes it's like I've got a herd of wild horses trying to break free out of me, trampling everything.'

'Try this,' I said, 'when you feel you're getting explosive: close your mouth and place your tongue on the roof of your mouth, then slowly and deeply breath through your nose. This will really help you transform that explosive feeling into a calmer, safer energy.'

We all tried it and I could feel the energy around us relax even more. Charlie now laid down on his side and let out a deep sigh as he placed his head on the ground.

'That sighing sound is your dog releasing the last of his pent-up stress,' I explained. 'See, what we're doing, it sounds like a simple thing to do, but we're actually practising a very powerful form of circular breathing. Chinese monks have been practicing Qi Gong for centuries.'

'So Charlie will let me know when my energy starts to get out of control because he'll start running around, barking?' asked Dean.

'Exactly,' I said. I love it when people start understanding how energy can dramatically change the behaviour of a dog — and a human.

The family promised to let me know how they got on.

I walked out the gate, took three deep cleansing breaths and shook my hands out so the residual energy from the consultation flicked off me and out of my system.

I'll never stop being grateful to the Chinese Qi Gong monks who knew so much about the power of breathing to control energy. If you have an issue with your energy levels then it's time to do something about it. Stop letting your overwhelming energy steamroll others.

Ultimately, the only person who can make you happy is you

I find people who are always miserable with everyone and everything around them simply don't like themselves much at all. I believe you can only find genuine, lasting happiness when you start to like and admire the person inside you — because that's the person you have to live with twenty-four hours a day for the rest of your life.

Fiona used to live in my neighbourhood and was extremely unhappy with everyone around her . She had two rescue dogs — both cute mongrels — and they were like two little temperature gauges, only instead of measuring how hot or cold it was outside, they couldn't help measuring Fiona's happiness or unhappiness levels.

You could always tell when she was happy. She'd be walking along and her two dogs would be bounding along at her side, grinning and panting, their tails waving along like banners in the air. As she'd get closer, you'd see her smiling and there would be a distinct bounce in her step.

However, most of the time when you'd see Fiona approaching, her dogs' behaviour would tell you a different story. They'd be padding along in an almost furtive manner, as far as possible from her as they could get, their tails down in a low, unhappy position. Their mouths would be closed and they'd occasionally lick their lips nervously. As soon as they'd see anyone they'd start barking and yapping nervously, standing in the middle of the footpath. They were obviously trying to protect their mistress when she was feeling weak.

When I first met Fiona in one of these miserable moods I asked her what was wrong. There was always a reason for her unhappiness. The house she'd recently bought wasn't as perfect as she'd hoped. Her lawn was tricky to mow. A neighbour's dog was howling at night, keeping her awake. The weather was either too hot or too cold. The rather rough roads were slowly wrecking her car. You name it, there was always a million and one reasons why she was unhappy.

I got sick of asking her what was wrong because it was always someone else who was responsible for making her unhappy. I never heard Fiona say one nice thing about any other person, her dogs, her house or the beautiful area she lived in. In fact, I never heard her say anything positive at all — even about herself.

It got to the point where her sadness was like a dark cloud that followed her around the neighbourhood. Even her dogs started staying out of close proximity to her, as though her unhappiness was toxic. One day I suggested she should perhaps go and seek help with her constant —

almost permanent — state of unhappiness but she became very upset and was insulted.

Eventually she moved away. The real estate agent who sold her property told me that he regularly met unhappy people like Fiona in his business.

'Oh sure, it's the unhappy people out there who keep on making us real estate agents plenty of money,' he chuckled. 'Because nobody moves around like an unhappy person. They think they're moving away from a problem neighbourhood or problem neighbours or whatever. The trouble is, it's really themselves they don't like so no matter how many times they move they never manage to escape.'

'Do you know how often Fiona's moved so far?' I asked.

The real estate agent winked. 'She told me this is the tenth time she's been forced to sell her house and move. Sounds like she doesn't like herself much at all, doesn't it?'

The memory of Fiona and her two cute mongrels always reminds me that if I'm really unhappy with the world around me then I'm probably not happy with myself at that moment. Maybe I'm not admiring or liking myself because I'm being selfish or pig-headed or disorganised or thoughtless. As I become unhappier with myself all that unhappiness just oozes out and infects how I see the rest of my life. However, the big test of whether I'm right or not is checking to see how my dogs are feeling around me. If they're unhappy even when we're all relaxing, then I'm at fault. Dogs are great at detecting whether you're happy with yourself or not.

Start taking responsibility for the decisions you make

The brutal truth is you can't keep blaming everyone else when things go wrong in your life — especially if the same problem occurs over and over again.

Denny was a busy web designer and spent long hours at her office. Although she was probably very responsible to her clients, when it came to Fergus, her teenage Irish Setter, she was one of the laziest owners I'd ever met. She called me out to advise her when she got a hefty fine from the local dog ranger for Fergus roaming freely around the neighbourhood. It quickly became clear to me that I was dealing with a problem owner, not a problem dog.

Fergus was a big, fit, energetic dog who needed a hell of a lot of exercise but wasn't getting any. As soon as he got bored and restless he'd hop the high fence and race down to the local school to play with the children. Sick of warning Denny to keep him at home, the ranger had finally slapped a hefty fine on her.

I outlined a simple exercise program for Denny to stick to that would fit in with her busy schedule and she promised to get Fergus out for two good walks every day. We also discussed ways to make her fence more escape-proof. However, there was something about the way Denny didn't quite meet my eyes that made me suspect she wouldn't do anything at all about exercising her poor dog.

To be honest, there's nothing that makes me more frustrated than seeing a really energetic dog jammed in a backyard virtually every day of its life.

As one week went past and then another, I couldn't help fretting about Fergus. Would that magnificent dog get the exercise he needed? Why had such a lazy person chosen such an energetic breed? I guessed Denny had picked Fergus for his silky, glowing red coat and his friendly, affectionate personality. I decided to ring her up and check on the situation.

'Oh yeah, bloody Fergus,' Denny said. 'He's cost me more money since I saw you. The damned ranger slapped another fine on me two days ago when he picked him up from the school. He got out over the fence again. He sure is proving to be an expensive dog.'

I took a deep breath to try to calm myself. 'And have you been exercising him as you promised you would?'

'Sure,' she said vaguely. 'Well, most days. I've been so busy lately. Lots of new clients. You know how it is.'

I could tell from her voice that she was lying. No doubt she hadn't exercised poor Fergus at all. No wonder the poor dog was jumping the fence — he'd decided to walk himself. I strongly reminded her of her promise to exercise him and again she promised she would.

Now I was deeply worried about Fergus's future. The poor dog was never going to get walked at all, let alone the two big walks he needed every day of his life.

I rang up a few more times and learned with a sinking heart of more fines piling up. From experience, I knew Fergus's days were numbered. Most owners reach a breaking point of how much they'll let a dog cost them before they get rid of it.

'How would you like it if I found a new home for Fergus?' I asked desperately during my next phone call.

'Nah, he's fine,' Denny said vaguely. 'Business is good — I can afford the bloody fines. But he's a pretty wilful dog, the way he keeps on escaping.'

I bit my tongue. I knew she was still lying about walking the dog.

I met up with the local dog ranger, Pete, and he said Denny was indeed a frustrating owner to deal with.

'It's always someone else's fault,' Pete said. 'You know the sort of owner. Two weeks ago it was the mail courier who left the gate open. Last week the neighbour next door apparently let him out because he got sick of the dog howling in the backyard. This week it was the local kids who walk past every day who apparently encouraged it to follow them.' He sighed. 'She just won't take any responsibility for this problem. Ultimately she has to deal with it.'

'I advised her she needed to invest in an escape-proof fence and told her she absolutely had to take him for two walks a day, every day, or he'd go stir crazy stuck in that small backyard.'

'We both know the type of owner she is,' he said. 'Doesn't matter what you say — they're never to blame for the consequences.'

I rang up the ranger one more time a few weeks later but he was away on his annual holidays. Another ranger I didn't know said that Fergus had finally been surrendered by his owner to the local council. When I rang up the pound I got an update on Denny's dog: Fergus had been bought by new owners from outside the local area, destination unknown.

I could only hope that his new humans would be better than Denny.

Take responsibility for the decisions you make in life. Accept that if you've got a messy problem that won't go away — like Denny's piling up dog fines — then realise the decisions you keep making are not helping the mess go away. Only when you start making wiser decisions will you watch familiar problems disappear.

2

What can dogs teach us about living a happier life?

If there's one thing I've always loved about dogs, it's that no matter how bad a situation gets they just seem to be able to bounce back. The way dogs' tails are so ready to start wagging for the slightest reason just shouts to the world how naturally optimistic they are.

Of course I'm not the only person inspired by their dog's unflagging happiness. So many people I've met over the years have told me that their dog is definitely one of the highlights in their life. Quite simply, I believe our dogs can teach us how to be happier.

Try to laugh out loud — even if you're squirming with embarrassment inside

Have you ever found yourself in a large group of people and embarrassed yourself in a truly humiliating way? The next time it happens to you, don't curl up in shame. Instead, handle the moment with dignity by seeing the humour in the situation and laugh along with the crowd.

Nobody has taught me this better than dogs. Here's a few dog blooper moments I've known.

Once I was a speaker at a huge pet expo and saw a lady get totally embarrassed by her dog. She'd just won a fancy championship trophy by guiding her dog around a difficult obstacle course helping him to take the fastest, best route, while he carried a little rubber dumbbell in his mouth. Before stepping up onto the podium to receive her huge gold cup in front of the politely clapping crowd, the lady asked her dog to drop the rubber dumbbell so she could hand it back to the steward. The dog, however, was so excited by all the attention he was getting from nearly a thousand people that he suddenly decided to rebel.

Just as the TV cameras zoomed in on the judge saying into the microphone, 'Without a doubt, ladies and gentlemen, this is one of the most wonderfully obedient dogs we have here today', the champion dog backed away from his owner, growling and shaking his head, refusing to release the dumbbell into her outstretched hand. The TV cameras and laughing crowd watched as the rebel dog kept backing away from his crimson-faced owner, then broke into a gallop, racing around the stage at top speed. We all watched as he held the rubber dumbbell high in the air. Clearly he saw it as his own personal trophy and he proudly completed three more victory laps of the stage. Then, feeling completely puffed up with his own sense of importance, he leaped into the crowd and started racing around the conference hall, much to the delight of the audience who laughed even louder.

I walked over to the dog's owner, whose eyes brimmed with tears of humiliation, and hugged her.

'My dog has *never* done anything like this before,' she said.

'Darling,' I said, 'there's only one thing you can do right now to keep your dignity, and that's join this crowd and laugh. That dog just proved he's cleverer than all of us here today — and there's absolutely nothing we can do about it except laugh along with the cheeky rascal.'

So she did laugh and she genuinely relaxed enough to enjoy the humour of the situation — she even clapped as her dog galloped past for several more laps around the stage. He made the news on TV that night and instead of a weeping, horrified owner we saw a lady laughing as her cheeky dog made damned sure absolutely everybody realised what a natural-born star he was.

Here's another time when my dignity was rescued by laughing. I was taking my three dogs for a walk without their leashes when a potential client I really wanted to impress pulled up in his car to say hello.

Feeling pretty good about myself, I started boasting about how well behaved my dogs were off-leash. As if on cue, a cheeky wallaby hopped past and — *whoosh!* — all three of my dogs shot past like hairy missiles. One dog even leaped straight over the car bonnet.

I stared after them as they disappeared into the gum trees. Wrestling with almost suffocating humiliation, I then had to turn back to the man roaring with laughter in his car. In that moment I saw there was only one way to take the humiliation: on the chin with a laugh.

'As you can see,' I said with a wry smile, 'I may have to tweak my training method here and there. Like making sure my dogs stay on their damned leashes around wallabies in future.'

The man was impressed by my calm acceptance of defeat and decided to let me train his dogs.

The funny thing is, once you make the decision to laugh at yourself in embarrassing situations you straightaway feel better. I call this 'tossing aside your ego'.

Finally, another humiliating moment where laughter saved my dignity happened in front of a TV camera. A pair of very small, fluffy white Chihuahuas decided during the filming of a TV interview that I'd been hogging the limelight quite enough for the day.

The interviewer and I were crouching down on our haunches beside the cute little dogs and the interviewer said warmly, 'Gee, Martin, you seem to have such an incredible affinity with dogs, why is this?'

Without any warning, the dogs leaped at each other and started fighting furiously. I pulled them apart, but they immediately started attacking my dreadlocks as though they were deadly snakes that had to be vanquished. Not wanting to hurt the tiny things, it took me a few moments to untangle them from my hair. Meanwhile, the interviewer, director, dogs' owner, cameraman and the sound man were all rolling around on the floor in hysterics.

Somehow, from the scattered remains of my pride, I managed to retrieve my sense of humour. 'I guess they don't like my hairstyle, huh?' I asked with a dry laugh.

Later the cameraman said I'd acted like a true star by not having a tantrum.

Dogs really know when to pick their moment to embarrass you — and it's always when there's an audience. Why? Most dogs love to stage their rebellious moments so they can test your leadership skills while you're weakened by embarrassment and usually when there's an audience watching — the bigger the audience, the better. So if your dog humiliates you in public just laugh along and admit defeat.

Having a sense of humour at a time like this proves you have true inner strength and natural, graceful dignity. Your dog and whoever else is watching will definitely be impressed by the way you keep your cool when you're embarrassed.

Are your negative emotions are trying to tell you something important?

Everyone feels sad, angry, frustrated and depressed sometimes — all those negative emotions that make us feel really lousy about ourselves. I've come to believe we should learn to be thankful for them for being powerful warning signals on our personal radar rather than fearing them. That's right — I believe they play an important part in helping us to find happiness. Think about it: aren't these emotions our body's ingenious way of sending us warnings that we need to make some drastic changes in our life?

Gerry was a professional dog groomer who owned a successful business in the city. He was having trouble with a few aggressive dogs at his fancy dog grooming salon and asked me to show him some natural dog calming techniques.

Afterwards, we were eating at a nearby café when a very expensively dressed young man walked in and kissed Gerry on the cheek. He looked me up and down.

'Goodness, lunching with the hairy barbarians,' he said with a smirk. 'Sorry to interrupt but I absolutely need to borrow from the Bank of Gerry again.'

I saw Gerry frown as he discreetly got out his wallet and handed the still-smirking man a fat wad of cash.

'Ta — I'm off to make myself pretty,' he said.

I'd seen people like the young man before and they usually meant trouble, especially for the person handing over the money.

'Who's that?'

Gerry sighed. 'That's Harry. The man I love and the reason I no longer sleep well at night.' He caught sight of my face and rolled his eyes. 'By that I mean I'm too sick with worry to sleep.'

'Why's that?'

'Harry is slowly bankrupting me,' Gerry said.

'Expensive habit,' I said.

Gerry's laugh was a bitter sound. 'Painfully expensive.' He pushed away his half-eaten pasta. 'Actually, I don't feel hungry any more.'

'You should start listening to your gut feelings more,' I warned him. 'Your body's obviously trying to tell you how unhappy you are, even though your brain's trying to block all your unhappiness out.'

'I'm not sure happiness and Harry go together,' he said. 'All I seem to feel these days is anxious when he's not with me because I worry about who he's with, depressed after I hand over money because I know he's taking advantage of me, and damned angry when I see all the bills flooding in. He's maxed out every single one of my credit cards.'

'So why are you still with him?' I asked. 'You should stop being so terrified of all those negative feelings inside you and start working out what they're trying to tell you. Each one of those negative feelings you have right now is telling you to get rid of him — that he's unhealthy for you.'

'We do have good times,' he protested.

'So what?' I asked. 'I mean, look at you — you can't even finish eating your lunch, you're still so upset about his behaviour just now.'

'I love him,' he said.

'You *want* to love him,' I corrected. 'Let's take your dogs for a walk so you can remind yourself what real love feels like.'

We were soon walking his two beautiful King Cavalier Spaniels, Sally and Saffy, around the nearby park that allowed dogs off-leash. Released, Sally and Saffy ran off in excitement then circled around and raced back to us, their tongues and ears flapping in the wind — the pure joy of being out with their favourite human in the world was totally unmistakable.

We laughed at the sight of them.

'That's how you and Harry should feel about each other,' I said. 'You should be working as a team, being happy, feeling like life's one hell of an adventure.' I looked at him. 'Unfortunately that's *not* what I saw when I watched the two of you together.'

Gerry stuck out his bottom lip in a stubborn way. 'But —'

Sally and Saffy ran over and paused, genuine affection sparkling in their eyes.

'Has Harry ever looked at you like that?' I asked. '*Ever?*'

Gerry's eyes softened as he looked down at his two beloved dogs. 'No — nobody's ever looked at me the way Sally and Saffy do,' he said.

'Well then,' I said, slapping him on the back. 'Dump the loser and find someone who loves you like Sally and Saffy do.'

'I'm not ready to give up on Harry yet,' he said. 'I've invested so much emotional energy in him and —'

I held up a hand to interrupt him. 'You've got to go home and face Harry again tonight. What does your gut say to that?'

He looked at me and sighed. 'It's twisting so much that I'm already feeling sick to the stomach,' he admitted.

'Your gut's telling you it's decision time,' I said bluntly. 'That man makes you physically ill.'

He looked into the distance — no doubt into a messy, argumentative future with a man who never stopped emotionally and financially abusing him. Then he looked down at Sally and Saffy, who were looking up at him with trusting, adoring eyes.

After a few minutes, he gave a sad laugh. 'I guess if I'm honest, my gut is telling me it's high time the Bank of Gerry finally foreclosed on Harry,' he said. 'I definitely deserve better.'

'Sure you do. You deserve a person who makes you feel as great as Sally and Saffy do,' I said. 'From now on use your dogs as your benchmark of what real love feels like.

If the new person in your life doesn't make you feel that happy — walk away. Learn to listen to your gut feelings.'

If you're having negative feelings don't be afraid of them and don't make the mistake of ignoring them or you'll make yourself sick. Instead, examine each negative feeling honestly and work out what changes they're telling you to make in your life. Only when you start making those changes, will you find the happiness you deserve.

Do you let one dark cloud cover your entire sky?

Are you a person who can shake off a bad moment or a bad day and get on with things? Or does any misfortune really throw you and make you believe that your whole life's an irretrievable mess? This story's about how your dog can teach you to shake off life's bad moments so you can move forward as quickly as possible. Remember, the sooner you move on, the sooner you can enjoy life again.

Barry was a big old black dog who had a white-flecked muzzle and loped along beside his human, Brett, as the two of them walked their familiar route around the village I lived in. Although Barry was a dog who was quite haughty with humans, he really liked meeting other dogs. In fact, as soon as he'd see another dog, he'd lope straight up to them and say a friendly hello by licking their faces exuberantly. Every dog he saw was a fantastic reason to be happy and excited.

The only problem was no other dogs liked Barry.

It was almost comical the way Barry would rush with delight to another dog — big tongue lolling out, fat tail wagging — then almost immediately get attacked by the other dog for his troubles.

Every single village dog had attacked Barry at some stage or another. Why? The truth was he had rather pushy, impolite dog manners — nobody appreciates getting licked all over the face by a virtual stranger — and the other dogs had no qualms about letting him know it. My own dogs just learned to ignore him and pretend he didn't exist.

But the thing that used to amaze me about Barry was the way he'd never be down in the dumps for long. After getting attacked, he'd be glum for a few moments — then he'd simply shake his rotund body until all that stress of being disliked shook straight off him.

By the time he rejoined Brett, he'd be back to his normal, optimistic self. Ready to enjoy the walk again — and more than ready to greet another unenthusiastic village dog.

Brett was the very opposite of optimistic. One small dark cloud would quickly grow and spread to cover the entire sky of his life. You've probably met people like that — maybe you tend to do it yourself.

For instance, one conversation I had with Brett went like this:

'Hi there, Brett. Beautiful evening, isn't it?'

'Yes, suppose it is, sort of.'

'You okay?'

'Ah, just thinking about the rotten day I had. Mechanic said I had to get new front tyres for my car today. It's really spoilt my whole day, thinking about those wretched, over-priced tyres.'

'Oh well,' I said. 'No point fretting about it.'

I tried to turn the conversation to something happier, but Brett just kept remarking on how much those 'wretched, over-priced tyres' were spoiling his day.

Finally I got so annoyed that I stopped and said, 'Brett — your dog Barry could teach you not to let one dark cloud cover your entire sky.'

I pointed to where Barry was running up to another village dog. Within seconds he'd gotten nipped smartly on the nose and was standing, looking glumly after the other dog as it trotted away.

'Watch this, Brett,' I said. 'If something horrible happens in your day, what do you do? Dwell on it endlessly, making it a hundred times more depressing? Or …?'

We watched Barry stand still and shake his body from the tip of his nose to the tip of his tail. When he stopped, his normal happy-go-lucky grin was back again. He loped up to us, everything in his world optimistic once more.

I turned to Brett. 'That's what you need to do — learn to shake off your bad moments so they don't sour the rest of your day. All dogs do that — it's their way of ridding themselves of any stress. Watch how often they shake themselves every day.'

Brett just looked at me uncomprehendingly. 'Sorry — what's that, Martin? I just can't seem to think about anything else at the moment while I've got those wretched, over-priced tyres on my mind.'

The next time you catch yourself sliding into pessimism when something bad happens, take a deep breath and be inspired by the way your dog shakes off bad moments to quickly emerge happy and optimistic again. Work out how to shake off your own pessimism. Does it help if you listen to great music? Watch a funny DVD? Go for a swim? Cook up a comfort snack? Take a brisk walk? Learn how you can best shake off that dark cloud from your shoulders.

Don't forget, you're having a bad moment or a bad day, just like everyone does. But let's face it — you can't let that relatively small cloud darken your whole sky or you're going to live a very cloudy life, aren't you?

Look to your dog to rethink everything you know about failing

Although it doesn't always feel like it at the time, every single failure in your life is another essential lesson that teaches you how to get better at what you really want to do. All the successful people I've met know failures and mistakes are a normal part of learning.

Nate was one young businessman who learned all his business failures were the stepping stones to success. However, it wasn't a business course that taught him this tough lesson — it was his dog.

Nate was twenty-eight when I first came out to help him with his huge six-month-old harlequin Great Dane pup, Bear, who was jumping up on people deliberately. Clearly, he was enjoying the way he could bring them crashing to the ground.

'Look at me — I'm a complete failure,' Nate confided to me after I showed him how to stop the problem within minutes. 'I'm even a failure at training my own dog.'

'What are you talking about?' I asked. 'You're a successful businessman. Look around — you're a rich, young man.'

'Martin, this is all inherited money. I'm what's known as a trust-fund baby. All I want to do is make my own money. But it's damned harder than it looks. I've started over five businesses and they've all failed spectacularly.' He told me how much they'd cost him and my eyes widened in shock. No wonder he was feeling so low about himself.

'But the worst thing is,' he said, 'it feels like I've got my stern, steely-eyed dad looking over my shoulder all the time. Every time another business venture fails, he doesn't say much, but his mouth tightens up. His eyes look at me as though I'm a complete write-off.'

For the first time I really started tuning in to what Nate was trying to tell me. Instead of thinking of him as a lucky rich kid with plenty of money to burn, I saw a young man who was now teetering right at the very edge. His self-esteem looked like it couldn't sink much lower.

Although he'd failed so spectacularly up to this point, I suddenly felt a surge of admiration for the guy. I mean let's face it, the guy could have spent the last ten years partying instead of working non-stop on his business ventures. What worried me were the four men hanging around his house. To me, they looked like ruthless, charming drug dealers. The sharks were obviously circling, waiting for this young man to have a complete meltdown so they could move in and help themselves to the rest of his fortune. Once they got him hooked on drugs it would be like taking candy from a baby.

I decided I couldn't sit back and let the sharks get him.

'You're worrying me, Nate,' I said. 'It's not healthy for anyone to think they're a complete failure, because when you start thinking like that you make yourself extremely vulnerable. You start making stupid decisions and, worse, you start flapping around like an idiot and that's when the sharks smell blood in the water and start circling.' I gestured over at his shady friends. 'Let's take a closer look at these so-called failures of yours.'

'My dad's right — I'm nothing but a complete business failure.'

'Well,' I said. 'What you call failure and I call failure are two different things. I actually see a young man who's never stopped trying to stand on his own two feet and find himself.' I let that sink in. 'I see a man who despite years of temptation never became lazy or buried himself in non-stop partying, drugs and alcohol.'

I noticed him sit up a little straighter.

'Let's be honest here, it's your dad who's really making you feel like a failure. Instead of giving you good advice he just stands in the background judging you and making you feel hopeless. Although he must seem pretty powerful to you, I reckon he's the real failure here — a failure at being a good father to you.

'As for your string of business failures — come over and watch Bear for a moment so you can put all your mistakes into some sort of perspective.'

We wandered over to watch his huge, clumsy Great Dane pup play-wrestling with the Kelpie who'd wandered over from next door. Despite the pup's much larger size, the

Kelpie was using his experience to easily out-manoeuvre, out-play and basically win the play-fight again and again.

I pointed this out to Nate. 'Look at the way Bear is learning to play-wrestle through making endless mistakes like these. Imagine how many games he's going to lose by the time he reaches adulthood. Thousands? Hundreds of thousands?' I paused. 'Get it? He's not failing — he's just learning.

'So why are you listening to your old man so much? I bet you he's not telling you about when he had his own arse soundly whipped by some bad business deal. If your dad won't be your teacher in business then you've got to go and find your own mentor who you can trust. Someone like that old Kelpie who'll keep teaching you whatever you need to know.'

I stayed in contact with Nate over the years and saw his career soar. Now that he saw he was still in his puppy stage of learning how to be a businessman, he focused more on learning all he could. He also asked for help much more and he found a few business mentors he could trust.

The biggest change in him was realising that he wasn't the failure he'd always thought he was. With his new confidence, he now looked forward at his goals instead of perpetually looking backwards at his mistakes. He tried out ideas — sometimes they worked and sometimes they didn't — but he never again called himself a failure.

Bear matured into a really calm, sensible, confident dog who was great fun. Nate became an extremely successful property developer. He became particularly respected by his peers for his calm acceptance of his mistakes and the way he smoothly moved forward to the next idea instead of wasting time having tantrums or meltdowns. Nate said his greatest mentor was a very enlightened individual called Bear.

Stop wasting your precious energy trying to control the uncontrollable

Wasting your time, talent and emotional energy on things that are beyond your control is a recipe for frustration and unhappiness.

One lady who saved her sanity by learning not to be a control freak was Annie. I met her through her rescue dog, Darcy. Annie was so worried about the behaviour of her Cattle Dog-cross-Labrador that she called me out after the vet couldn't find anything physically wrong with him.

'He's acting very strange lately,' Annie told me on the phone. 'He's sulking a lot — as though he's really depressed or something. I'm concerned by the way he's ignoring us all.'

When I arrived at Annie's house, I heard loud, raised voices.

'Uh, sorry,' said Annie when she opened the door at last. 'We're having a bit of a family crisis at the moment but don't worry — I'll tell everyone to shut up while we work out what's going on with Darcy.'

It didn't take long before I learned why there was so much turmoil going on in the household. Annie's grown-up daughter, Karen, was having a marriage breakdown because she'd caught her husband having an affair. Annie was getting extremely frustrated with her husband, Ian, for not being more outraged on their daughter's behalf. Karen wanted a divorce without any anger and wanted her controlling mum to butt out of her business.

I glanced down at Darcy. This wise four-year-old Cattle Dog-cross was simply lying in a corner of the room, facing the wall, his chin on the floor, ears down and eyes shut.

Annie strode across to me. 'Well, what do you think is wrong with him, Martin?' she asked, concerned. 'The vet can't find anything wrong with him and look at the other two young dogs — they're perfectly fine.'

I looked at the dogs as they raced around the room, barking and chasing each other in a mad frenzy and generally adding to the noise level of the family fight. They weren't fine at all. In fact, they were acting in a very stressed, manic manner.

'Is Darcy depressed?' asked Annie in genuine concern.

'No — Darcy's gone into full survival mode. He's obviously your lead dog and as everything in your house is whirling totally out of control, he's simply doing his best to shut down from the situation.'

'Huh?' asked Annie.

'Look at him,' I said. 'He's done whatever he can to shut off all this chaos. He's shut down his ears, his eyes and his body.'

'Is he okay?'

'He's very stressed but he's okay,' I said. 'He's actually doing the sensible thing. If he didn't shut down like this he'd wind up having a nervous breakdown.'

'I know how *that* feels,' Annie said grimly. 'I'm having a nervous breakdown right now trying to fix everything going wrong in this family. Not that anyone's appreciating it.'

I looked at her, then down at poor Darcy. 'Maybe we could step out and take Darcy for a walk around the block and get a breath of fresh air.'

'Okay,' she said.

Within moments we were walking down the leafy street and I watched in pleasure as both Darcy and Annie seemed to unwind, relax and start enjoying the simple, unexpected walk.

'Annie, can I be honest with you?' I asked after a while. '*Very* honest?'

'Okay,' she said uncertainly.

'It's obvious you love your family very much.'

'Sure I do,' she said a little defensively. 'I just want what's best for them. To help my kids and husband and grandkids to be happy.'

'I'm wondering if all that love and worry of yours is turning you into a bit of a control freak. I'm going to be honest here — what I saw back there was not a healthy environment, not for Darcy or your family or especially you. If you try to fix all the things that are beyond your control, you're going to go stark raving mad.'

She half laughed, half sobbed. 'Guess you're right, Martin — I feel physically sick with nerves these days.'

'From now on,' I said, 'be more like Darcy. When things happen in your family that you can't control — like your daughter's emotions — just detach from the chaos until it all settles down again.'

'What? Lie in the corner and close my ears and my eyes?' she asked.

'No, Darcy just did that because he was stuck in the house and couldn't escape. Just do what we're doing now —

get out, take a break from all those problems you can't fix, get some fresh air and take a walk. As you take a good, long walk you'll find that panicky desire to control everything around you start to slip away.'

'I won't promise you anything,' Annie said, 'but I'll try. I certainly can't go on the way I've been going or I'll end up in a mental asylum.'

'Good girl,' I said. 'And remember to watch Darcy. He'll be your warning system. When he goes and lies facing the wall then he's going into survival mode by shutting down all his senses. When he does that you know you're sliding back into a control-freak mumma again. As soon as you see that dog lie down in that anxious way, grab him and take both of you off on a good, healing walk.'

I held her hand and drew her to a stop. 'Remember — even with all the best intentions, you can't control everything in the world or fix it.'

If you suspect you're a closet control freak take your dog straight out for a healing walk and feel the panic, fear and helplessness fall off your shoulders with every step. Trying to control everything in your world — even for the very best reasons — will send you and everybody else around you totally bonkers.

Right now — add a small dash of pleasure to your life!

Someone sent me an email recently that read: 'Right now — add a small dash of pleasure to your life!' Thinking it sounded pretty damned corny, I deleted it with a snort.

But as I went about the rest of my day a funny thing happened. Wherever I went, whatever I was doing, I couldn't get the blasted sentence out of my head. I kept catching myself looking around thinking, 'Hmm ... how could I go about adding a dash of pleasure to my life right now?' Then, before I could stop myself, I made an extra little bit of effort to add a small, unexpected dash of pleasure to my day. Surprisingly enough, there always seemed to be some small way I could make my life just a little bit sweeter right there and then.

It might be simple and cost nothing. For example, I might make the effort of switching the car radio off and play one of my favourite CDs instead. That way my dash of pleasure was singing my head off to the music instead of listening to depressing news headlines. Or it could cost a little bit extra but be worth it. For example, instead of settling for a bland drive-thru greasy hamburger for lunch, I'd actually make the effort to drive an extra few blocks, find a park and sit down at my favourite Thai restaurant to enjoy a healthy and beautifully presented meal. Or instead of coming home and flopping into an armchair in exhaustion, I'd make an extra effort to freshen up with a shower, using an expensive sandalwood soap, then hang my hammock on the verandah and lie back feeling spoilt and pampered. That extra dash of luxurious comfort was so worth it.

Very soon, I found myself getting very good at treating myself to lots of lovely dashes of pleasure in my life.

Curious about how such small things made me so happy, I thought about what these dashes of pleasure really were. Most involved adding something special that would wake up my senses more than usual. It made me realise how often our senses shut down as we go about our normal work week. Even on the weekend we're usually too exhausted to kick-start our poor senses back into action. However, now I was keeping my senses alive and aware in all sorts of small ways throughout the week, I was much happier. The more my senses were kept awake the happier I felt.

I believe dogs are so happy because all their senses stay permanently alert. The only depressed dogs I've known have deliberately shut down all their senses. So I suggest you try this surprisingly effective tonic for your senses right now — add a dash of pleasure to your life!

3

What can dogs teach us about problem-solving?

Wherever I go, I love watching dogs, especially when they're trying to get a human or another dog to do what they want. In other words, they have a problem — 'How can I get this human to do what I want?' — and they keep trying out different solutions until they get the best result they can.

We've all seen dogs in action solving this problem. How can I get this human to pat me? How can I get that human to give me some of that yummy food? How can I grab everyone's attention right now? How can I grab control of this dog walk? How can I get away with jumping up on the couch? Believe me — dogs can be extremely creative at solving any problem if it means they'll get their own way!

Sometimes be still enough to hear that wise voice deep inside you

During my years of helping my clients with their dogs I've met people who jam-pack their lives with so many things that my head just swims at the thought of it. Basically, they make damned sure that every single hour of the day is filled with non-stop activity.

These really busy — and I do mean manically busy — people deliberately do everything they can to avoid being still and doing nothing. Why? Because when you stop *doing* you're left with stillness and when you're still, you feel.

Madeline called me because her seven Cocker Spaniels were really testing her ability to control them around the house. As soon as I walked inside the picket fence of her Queenslander home, an avalanche of Cocker Spaniels descended the wooden staircase and swarmed around my feet.

I gave them natural relaxing dog signals and they soon kept a polite, respectful distance from me. However, Madeline and her husband, John, weren't so lucky when they appeared on the verandah. The seven dogs turned, ran and leaped all over their owners, licking, nipping, barging and being extremely disrespectful. I sensed straightaway that there was a very manic undercurrent going on in this household.

I've seen thousands of normal, disrespectful dogs over the years who just haven't been taught polite manners but then there are dogs like these Cocker Spaniels, who were obviously so stressed and manic they were on the edge of a nervous breakdown. The incredibly intense energy radiating off these dogs told me there were some very dark, painful emotions being suppressed in this household.

Since none of my behaviour programs can begin to work until we get to the root of the human problem, I decided to plunge straight in.

'I have to be honest, Madeline and John,' I said as they welcomed me. 'Your home's beautiful — you both seem like lovely people — but the energy coming off these Cocker Spaniels tells me that we've got some dark, painful stuff going on here.'

A fleeting flash of pain flickered in Madeline's eyes, then disappeared behind her calm, polite mask. John sat up straighter and defensively stuck his jaw out a little.

'Excuse me — but I don't think our family is any of your business, Martin. We just called you out to help us with our dogs. They're —'

I held up my hand. 'Everything you're about to say about the dogs is merely symptoms,' I said firmly. 'Jumping up, nipping, barking, barging — blah, blah, blah — I know what you're going to say.' I paused. 'However, I can tell by the absolutely manic, out-of-control way they're behaving that there's a hell of a lot of suppressing of emotions going on in this household.

'I really can help your dogs,' I said. 'But I can't do anything until we get to the truth of the matter. It's time to come clean. What the hell's going on here? What's the big dark secret that you're both trying so hard to hide from me, yourselves, and the rest of the world?'

Madeline's shoulders slumped and she touched John on the hand as he was about to erupt in outrage. 'I trust Martin, John. I'm going to tell him the truth.'

I saw in relief that John's shoulders slumped as well. The sooner we got to the heart of the problem, the sooner we could start fixing it.

Madeline started trembling and took a deep, shuddering breath. 'The truth is — the truth is —'

'Our son is a heroin addict,' said John. When he lifted his eyes to mine I saw they were wretched beyond belief. 'Marcus lives in the city and he refuses to go to rehab. We've tried everything we can to help him, but he won't listen.'

'We're so ashamed — we've failed him obviously,' said Madeline. 'Now John and I keep ourselves as busy as we can. That way we don't leave ourselves any time to think. These darling Cocker Spaniels help keep me so busy that I hardly have any time and energy left to think about Marcus.'

John touched her hand. 'We tend to keep suppressing all our anger and pain and guilt under a polite veneer. None of our friends, family, neighbours — nobody suspects a thing.'

'Unfortunately, it's all this secrecy that's causing the dogs to really act out in this crazy, manic way,' I explained. One of the dogs came sniffing around me and I fondled its ears calmly. 'Dogs are such incredibly sensitive creatures — they pick up every bit of tension in a household and absorb it into themselves.

'Because you've suppressed all those painful, intense emotions, these dogs have absorbed so much stress and tension that it's now just exploding out of them. They've simply reached stress saturation point.'

'Oh, the poor darlings,' said Madeline.

'If the dogs are acting out even more than usual then I'm guessing there's been a new development in your relationship with Marcus recently.'

'I just visited him last week and it wasn't a success,' John said. 'We exchanged bitter words. I'm guessing the dogs are picking up the new level of tension.'

I nodded in agreement. 'Dogs feel every shift in emotions and as your stress levels rise, their chaotic behaviour increases too.'

'What on earth are we going to do?' Madeline asked.

'We've already started by opening up and airing your feelings. You've got to stop that dangerous habit of suppressing your emotions. Be honest with yourselves and with your son about how you're really feeling deep inside. Stop burying your feelings behind that polite mask, pretending that nothing's wrong. More importantly, stop being so hectically busy.'

'That's going to be particularly hard for me,' admitted Madeline.

'You need to start unwinding — walking, swimming, exercising — so you can stop feeling all that unhelpful restlessness inside you. Then you need to simply spend some time being still and quiet. It's going to be really hard for you both going quiet and letting all your painful emotions flood through you but you have to feel all that pain. Only then are you both going to be able to face the raw, brutal truth of your situation and understand how you got to this point in your life.'

I sat back. 'We all have a wise voice inside of us and once we have a chance to be still we can hear what it advises us to do next. I believe that two sensible, intelligent people like you are going to be able to work out how to help Marcus, but only when you start being honest and open about your feelings.

'How about I leave it at that now and we start discussing a program for the dogs?'

We spent the rest of the visit concentrating on a simple relaxation program for the dogs to help calm them down and teach them respectful manners.

Nine months later, Madeline rang me and it was a very emotional phone call. She and John had followed my suggestions and had found that inner stillness I'd suggested they look for. They'd listened to the wise voices inside them and had contacted Marcus again but this time with a new, more honest approach. They'd admitted to their son their part in causing him to become an addict. They asked him to consider rehab in the light of their new, more honest relationship and he'd agreed. He was now clean of drugs and continuing with the rehab's support program. The seven Cocker Spaniels were doing wonderfully well.

If you're keeping hectically busy to try to forget difficult emotions of fear, anger and sadness, ask yourself if suppressing these emotions is really helping your situation. Once you find your stillness, I think you'll hear an inner voice that will advise you how to finally solve the problem you've been trying to suppress for so long.

Are you stopping yourself from feeling by burying yourself in drugs or alcohol?

I haven't touched alcohol now for over ten years and I've encouraged many others to stop drinking if it doesn't agree with them.

One lady I encouraged to give up alcohol was Molly, who had four rescue dogs and it was for the sake of her beloved dogs that she stopped drinking.

Molly was a laughing, happy, kind lady — when she was sober. She had four gorgeous mongrels who adored her — again, when she was sober. She called me out for a consultation every time she adopted a new dog to help it become accepted into her pack. She'd always welcome me with a clean house, a beautifully cooked lunch and plenty of funny stories. However, I could always feel a quiet sense of desperation under her surface happiness. One day I asked her if she was okay and she breezily waved off my question.

'Ah, I'm as happy as a lark these days. Used to be married to a fellow but he decided to run off one day with a much younger lady. Well, what can you do? That was six years ago. But I've got my four sweetie-pies around me now and dogs never let you down, do they?'

I agreed with her about the loyalty of dogs and left the subject alone.

One day she rang me up in tears. She'd broken both her legs and was wondering if I could help her by babysitting her four dogs while she recovered in hospital and then moved to her sister's house.

I agreed, but before I went to pick up the dogs from her house, I dropped in to the hospital to visit her and to pick up her house keys. She looked terrible. Her eyes were red and bleary. She was covered in scratches. Her skin was pasty.

'What on earth happened?' I asked. 'How did you manage to break *both* your legs?'

'Oh, you know,' she said airily. 'Some little tranquilliser pills and a cask of wine to wash it all down with. Then I took the express route down the stairs — head first. You might as well know, Martin — I'm a drunk and a pill-popper. Guess I didn't take my husband leaving me as well as I might have pretended. I've been getting drunk every single night since he left six years ago.'

'Promise me you'll stop,' I said. 'While you're in hospital, get help. It's time to stop burying all those painful feelings about being abandoned by your husband. You won't find any real relief in alcohol and tranquillisers. They'll just make things worse.'

'Know what? Might actually be able do it,' she said. 'You know why? Because of those four darling sweetie-pies of mine. Doctors said I was smoking last night before my accident and left a cigarette burning on the armrest of my chair. Could easily have started a fire and my dear babies would have been killed because I lock the doors at night. They wouldn't have been able to escape.' She patted my hand. 'I'm a loyal kind of person and I want to repay my dogs for their unwavering loyalty to me. I'll talk to the doctor today about rehab. I'll give it a go because I love those dogs, Martin — I really do.'

I gave her a warm hug. 'Time to start loving yourself again, Molly, so you can look after yourself and those great dogs of yours. I won't say anything more because you know what you have to do.'

Molly's been sober for six years. Her rescue dogs still adore her.

Stop making excuses right now!

I was at a client's house about a dog problem but the consultation wasn't going well. I struggled on.

'I love my dog,' said the young man, Billy. 'He's the greatest dog in the world.'

'I'm glad to hear that,' I said, 'because the solution to this problem is going to include you taking Rusty for two walks a day — and I mean *every* single day. Rusty needs plenty of exercise to be calm and well behaved.'

Billy and his father, George, had called me because their teenage dog Rusty kept barking when they went out and the neighbours were beginning to complain. As part of the solution I said they had to walk him twice a day in a very regular routine. George said he couldn't because he had an injured back.

I looked at Billy and watched his face shut off. It was obvious he didn't want to walk Rusty either.

'There's no good places to walk your dog around here,' he said.

'What are you talking about?' I said. 'This is one of the most beautiful parts of the world — this is a fantastic place to walk your dog.'

'There's no footpath, the dirt lanes are too rough to walk along.'

'I hope you're kidding,' I said in disgust. I couldn't believe this was a 22-year-old young man giving me these pathetic excuses. 'You only need to walk the dog up the lane and back. Once in the morning and once in the afternoon. That's all. It's not much to repay your dog for all his love and loyalty.'

Billy's eyes shifted about and then settled back on me. 'Well ... I actually don't have much time in the morning to go on a walk.'

'Get up an hour earlier,' I said grimly.

The excuses continued to pour out of his mouth: 'I'm not feeling very fit at the moment'; 'I'm not sure if I can actually manage walking the entire length of the lane and back again'; 'I have some stuff I want to do at the moment so I'm going to be pretty busy.'

My ears finally shut off. I looked at his father but George just seemed to find his son's pitiful excuses normal too. Birds of a feather flock together; the thought flashed into my mind as I looked at this incredibly lazy father and his son. It was obvious that making excuses was Billy's natural response to anything that was even slightly difficult. I realised I was bored by both of them. It would be easier to roll a snowball through hell than get this pair to walk their dog.

Here was this handsome, healthy dog looking up at his humans so eagerly that he was inspirational to watch. All that wonderful dog wanted to do was get out into the fresh air and explore the world — and this lump of a young man and his equally lazy father couldn't even walk him to the end of the lane twice a day. They just wanted to surf the TV channels in their spare time.

I stood up but father and son were already staring at their vast wide-screen TV. Only Rusty bothered walking me to the door. He looked longingly outside and hopefully back at his owners but they were still mesmerised by the TV.

'Sorry, boy,' I said. 'But these humans are just too lazy for me to budge. Nothing I say is going to get them off their lazy butts to get you the exercise you need.' I felt a heavy cloud of guilt as I walked back up the lane to where I'd parked my car.

Rusty was desperately in need of lots of exercise every single day and unfortunately he'd been taken on by two of the laziest men I'd met in a while.

A week later I rang up George and Billy with a proposal: I'd found a new home for Rusty with a healthy young woman who loved to run along the beach every day.

'Oh no,' said George in outrage. 'I couldn't possibly give up Rusty, we love him too much.'

Three weeks later I rang up again to see how Rusty was going. I was still worried about his problem of barking when George and Billy went out. Billy answered the phone and I felt my jaw clench when I heard his lazy voice answer.

But in answer to my query about Rusty, he went quiet. Then he said, 'I'd better get Dad to tell you.' My heart went cold.

'Rusty was barking so much that, well, we had to let him out of the house and go free when we went shopping last Thursday,' George said. 'The neighbours had been complaining again, really kicking up a fuss. We let him have his freedom outside and he ran off into the bush. It's been — um — five days and he hasn't returned yet.'

There was a reason for that and we both knew it.

My gut twisted in icy dread. Now the cold weather had set in, the local farmers had put down lots of 1080, the special poison used for keeping the wild dog and dingo population to a minimum. There was no doubt that Rusty had picked up a poison bait out in the bush. His death would have been horrible and painful.

I couldn't speak, I was too angry and upset. I quietly replaced the phone receiver and stood staring at my wall for a moment.

George and Billy had been too lazy to build that beautiful, magnificent, generous-hearted dog a pen so he wouldn't go wandering off into the bush and take a bait. Neither had they bothered taking him for one decent walk since they'd brought him home, so he barked in frustration. In fact, they hadn't listened to one bit of advice I'd given them to help that dog — and now poor Rusty was dead.

Meanwhile those two lazy slobs who'd owned him sat in front of their wide-screen TV in complete comfort on their leather couch.

As usual it was a dog who paid the price for the endless excuses of humans.

Rusty, you were a magnificent dog.

Rest in peace.

Ask for help when you know you need it

Are you a person who finds it difficult to ask for help? Karen was a lady I met who really had problems asking for help when she obviously needed it — until her rescue dog, Emma, taught her to swallow her pride and fear and accept the grace of being offered help.

I met Karen when I was in a shopping mall car park. I'd finished my shopping and was getting in my car when I heard a curse, then a loud crash and glass breaking. I looked around and saw a woman staring down in horror at her shopping trolley, which had fallen over, the shopping bags inside it spilling their contents across the tarmac. Broken glass and spilt food spread around her.

'I'll help,' I offered.

We loaded what could be saved back into bags. Then Karen was even more horrified to find she'd locked her keys inside the car. She burst into tears. 'I can't take any more.'

'I'll take you home so you can get your spare set of keys and bring you back. It's okay,' I said. 'I'm not in any hurry — come on.'

In the car she apologised for her tears. She grimaced. 'Usually I'm okay but this month everything seems to be getting on top of me. My husband's just started working away from home and won't be back for another two months. My three kids seem to be all going through the worst bits of adolescence at the same time. I think I just found white ants in my house and my boss at work is away, so I'm being swamped with extra tasks. And now the bloody trolley's fallen over and killed a week's worth of groceries.' She gave me a faint smile. 'Sorry — you don't need to know all that, do you?'

I shrugged and grinned at her. 'It sounds like a nice bit of healthy venting if you ask me.'

We arrived at her home and were greeted by a gorgeous snowy-white mongrel.

'That's Emma,' Karen said, bending down and patting the dog's head and ears gently. 'She's such an adorable thing. Not a bad bone in her body. Can you believe some bastard dumped her on the side of the road? I saw him do it — then drive off. I pulled over and poor darling Emma trotted over

to my car and looked up at me with those beautiful eyes —
almost like she was begging me to help her. She's been with
us ever since. That was four years ago. She's brought us so
much pleasure and happiness. Weird to think that anyone
wanted to throw her away.'

She let herself inside to get her spare car keys while
I waited on her verandah, getting to know the very sweet
Emma better.

There was a loud curse from inside.

Yet another disaster had happened for poor Karen: a
water pipe had broken and there was a growing lake of water
spilling from her bathroom into the hallway. I switched off
the water at the mains and returned to find Karen sitting at
her table, completely falling to pieces.

'I just can't do all this on my own any more,' she said.
'But my husband really needs to take this new job working
away from home for the next few months. I can't ask him to
come back.'

'Then you're going to have to ask your family, friends
and neighbours for help,' I said. 'Otherwise you're going to
end up having a nervous breakdown.'

'I find it so damned *hard* to ask for help,' she admitted.

'You accepted my help today,' I reminded her.

She laughed. 'I didn't actually *ask* for your help. You just
steamrolled me into being helped.'

'Why is that such a problem?'

'Heaven knows. Fear? Pride? All I know is that I
absolutely *hate* asking for help.'

I looked at her, then her dog. 'Well, what about Emma,
here?'

She frowned. 'What about Emma?'

'What would have happened to her if she hadn't come and asked for your help that day she got dumped on the side of the road?'

'Is this your way of getting me to finally make a few phone calls and ask for help?'

'It's not so different, is it? Emma genuinely needed help and something inside you answered that.'

I stroked Emma's silky head. 'People like feeling good about themselves. Maybe not everyone can help you, but it's not shameful to ask. I see helping someone who genuinely needs it — who's completely vulnerable and isn't trying to take advantage of anyone — as a beautiful act of grace. Just calmly explain your situation and suggest how they could help. Whether they say "yes" or "no", you can thank them. It's as easy as that.'

'Or as difficult as that,' Karen muttered. 'Okay — I'll give it a go. Pass me the phone, will you? And that diary there.'

I sat outside and waited in the sun while she rang up friends, family and neighbours and got the help she so desperately needed.

Some time later she came out with Emma at her side and smiled shakily at me.

'Well — I'm not sure whether I feel humiliated, ashamed, guilty, relieved or just plain exhausted,' she said. 'But I've asked for help and everyone was surprisingly supportive. Whenever I felt my hands and voice start to tremble, I just patted darling Emma here and she gave me the strength to keep on ringing and asking for help.'

We both looked at Emma. I couldn't help being warmed by her happy eyes and cheerful, optimistic grin.

'My gran was right,' said Karen, turning her face up to catch the last of the sun. 'What goes around, comes around — and that includes a helping hand.'

She rested a grateful hand on Emma's head.

Learn how to deal with someone trying to start a fight

One thing dogs have taught me is how to avoid getting into a fight.

For years I'd allowed troublemakers to rub me up the wrong way, and before you could say 'Irish', I'd be launching straight into a humdinger, punch-up fight. Since I was a kid, I'd always thought walking away was the coward's way out.

Then I met Paddyboy, a beautiful red Pit Bull puppy. His owner was moving into rental accommodation that didn't allow pets and as no-one was willing to take on such a controversial breed, this pup was an hour away from euthanasia when I stepped in and adopted him.

Now, I'd never recommend anyone own a Pit Bull as they need an extremely knowledgeable, experienced and responsible owner who understands dog language and all the subtle ways dogs earn the right to dominate others. Paddyboy, however, grew up to be a truly wise and gentle-natured example of the breed. In fact, it was amazing to watch how much this dog would do to avoid a fight.

Much bigger and more aggressive dogs would run up to him on his leash and would growl and menace him. He'd simply stay relaxed and uninterested. He'd slowly raise his chin, look away slightly and slowly blink his eyes to relax his challengers. It was his way of saying that he wasn't afraid — and he didn't want to fight either. More importantly, he'd be giving off such calm signals that the other dog would find its adrenaline was being switched off naturally and within minutes, the other dog would wander off in confusion.

What he wouldn't do was stare straight at his attacker — either angrily or fearfully — knowing that this would just feed the adrenaline of the other dog and get it even more pumped up. He certainly wouldn't step closer and glare at his opponent, growling, snarling and threatening.

Watching Paddyboy refuse to fight, honestly taught me how weak I'd been up to this point. A strong leader, he taught me, is the one who chooses whether it's worth fighting or not. It's actually just weakness to allow yourself to be sucked into a fight that someone else starts.

Paddyboy also taught me that it's absolutely pointless fighting unless you have no alternative and someone's life is in real danger. Fighting for any other reason is just a mix of vanity, ego and pride.

So if you have a wild temper and you find yourself answering every stupid challenge thrown at you, think of wise Paddyboy. Do as he did. Raise your chin, act calm, aloof and uninterested and don't pump up your opponent's adrenaline by getting into a face-off situation. Confuse all challengers by explaining happily that you're too peaceful and content to bother wasting time fighting and politely say goodbye.

Is it cowardice to walk away from a challenge? Believe me, looking at Paddyboy — this beautiful, magnificently muscled dog who loved his daily walks — you could never accuse him of being a coward. He just happened to be so confident and happy in his own skin that he simply had no wish to fight anyone.

Sometimes it's better to think instinctively instead of rationally

When we face a tough decision, we're usually urged to sit down and think long and hard about what the smartest, most sensible thing is to do. In other words, we're encouraged to make a rational choice. However, I think the best decisions I've made in my life have actually been made by listening to my gut feelings, in other words, my instincts. Let's talk about thinking instinctively rather than rationally when it comes to making really big life-changing decisions.

Megan was a woman I knew who made one of the biggest decisions in her life by learning from her dog to listen to her instincts.

Recently divorced, Megan always walked her dog, Danny, around the same city park that I did. We often walked our dogs a few laps together and fell into conversation. Megan worked in the computer sales industry, had a well-paid, steady job and was comfortably off. She had three children and had stayed friends with her ex-husband. Yet despite how well she was doing, she admitted how dissatisfied she felt with her life.

One day, as we tramped around another lap of the leafy inner-city park, she told me how restless she was feeling. She threw a tennis ball really hard for Danny to retrieve and I got the idea that she'd like to throw a lot of other things from her life as well.

'You'd better talk about it,' I said, 'or you're going to explode. I can feel all that suppressed frustration inside you. Come on — what is it you really want?'

'Martin, I'm not sure what's exactly wrong with my life. All I know is there's something vaguely wrong with *everything* in it at the moment — everything except my kids and dog.'

'Maybe you need to make a big change — shake things up a bit so you feel like you're making a new life for yourself after the divorce?'

'I guess that's it,' she said. 'I feel like I'm not moving on and I'm just keeping the tattered pieces of my former life sticky-taped together.'

'Sounds like it's decision time. How do you really want to live your life?'

Megan looked at me. 'You're going to think I'm crazy but I really want to start a whole new lifestyle. Buy us a beach house up the coast where it's cheaper. Get out of the city and surround myself with the beauty and freedom of the bush. Get out of my stale, boring job. Maybe even retrain and try a whole new career.'

'I sure can picture that,' I said.

'It sounds so easy, doesn't it? *Just go and do it!* If only it was that easy. But life isn't a pretty magazine article. The reality is it would be total *madness* for me to leave a safe and steady job and head for the unknown at the moment.'

We continued tramping around the park. I watched Danny and my two dogs as they raced happily around the park, no worries on their mind except how they could wrestle the tennis ball off each other. Dogs don't use a rational mind to carefully plan out their futures. They live from moment to moment, listening only to their instincts — and I suspect they're a whole lot happier for it.

I thought of all the big decisions I'd made in my own life and they'd all been chosen because I'd listened to my instincts, and to be honest, there weren't many decisions I regretted.

I stopped and turned to Megan. 'I think when it's such a big decision you should listen to your instincts, your gut feeling,' I said carefully. 'I think when we start listening to our body — especially our gut — we're really listening to our deepest, most secret desires. I believe it's only when we obey our instincts that we find our greatest, deepest happiness.

'Instead of listening to all those sensible, safe arguments going on in your head, I think you should tune more into your instinctive, animal side. Try noticing how your body responds to each option. As you visualise each lifestyle, does your body tense up? Relax? Does your gut feel happy? Or does it feel like it's twisting around in misery? I think if you start listening to your body, you'll know which lifestyle will make you the happiest.'

She looked at our three dogs still playing together. 'I guess Danny always does look pretty unstressed, doesn't he? I might try listening to my gut feelings after all, Martin.'

Not long after that conversation I moved, and no longer walked my dogs in that park. Every now and then I wondered if Megan had taken the plunge, listened to her gut feeling and moved north to her beach-bush paradise or if she'd listened to her sensible brain and stayed in her safe inner-city life.

Then one day I received a postcard. It showed a bush-lined, white sand beach up north. On the reverse side was a short message:

> *Hi Martin,*
> *Took kids and Danny up for a weekend and ran along the beach and we all listened to our gut feelings. Felt overwhelmingly good! That's why we made the move!*
> *Love Megan.*

I believe when it comes to solving problems, we don't listen enough to what our own body is trying to tell us — especially our gut. If you feel restless and frustrated with your life at the moment and don't know what to do about it, why don't you try picturing your own dream lifestyle as you tune into how your body reacts? Listening to your body might give you the necessary courage to follow your own vision of deep happiness.

4

What can dogs teach us about our careers?

As dogs were domesticated and trained by us to become some of our most useful tools, I believe they really understand the importance of having a job.

Is your dog's job to hunt? Kill rats? Herd livestock? Guard your property? Retrieve game? Track the scent of something? Pull a sled? Protect you from enemies? Or just be a great companion for you? Whatever your dog's breed, it was designed to do a specific job and there's a very strong voice inside its head urging it to work, work, work! Unfortunately, not many dogs get a chance to follow the career they were bred for these days. However, I do feel there are some very interesting lessons dogs can still teach us about our careers.

I believe nobody understands better than your dog about being highly ambitious and wanting to become the leader of the pack, in other words, the Big Boss. Your dog knows that in a dog-eat-dog world, you're going to have to survive plenty of challenges, contests, duels, intrigues and complex politics on your ambitious climb to the top.

Here are a few ingenious tips I believe dogs can teach us about advancing in our careers.

Love what you do to excel

There's one thing I've always noticed about dogs who have a great talent or skill: they just love doing it! I believe the same holds true for people. They say that to master a skill you need to practise it for ten thousand hours or more. That means if you want to excel at something then you'd damned well better enjoy doing it!

Sophie was inspired by her father's talented sheep dog to stick to the career that she loved doing — even when times got tough. A keen student, Sophie had once had lofty dreams of editing Academy Award movies and had worked extremely hard, getting qualifications in film editing with honours. However, on graduation, she met with a brick wall — the film industry was totally uninterested in yet another film-editor graduate. She gamely contacted every agency and film production company in the country, but zilch.

I met her at her parents' country property one weekend when she was twenty-two. Nine months of pointless job searching was really getting her down. She was working as a cashier at a health food store, still chasing every film editing lead that came her way but so far without success.

I had lunch with Sophie and her parents on the verandah, and she told us about her latest job-search efforts.

'There just doesn't seem to be any openings anywhere. They don't even want to know about me even though I'll work for free! Even the work experience positions are filled to overflowing!'

Her dad, Lindsay, patted her hand. 'Don't give up, my girl. Something'll turn up. A career is forever — you've been looking for less than a year.'

'Yeah,' she muttered. 'And next year there will be a fresh crop of film editor graduates flooding the industry.'

Her mother said quietly, 'Perhaps you should retrain for a different career, darling? Perhaps something that has more employment opportunities. Computers? You were always brilliant at handling computers.'

'You're probably right,' said Sophie, 'But hell! I love film editing. I mean I *really* love it! I just can't imagine not doing it.'

I decided to keep quiet. I've always believed in following your dream career no matter what the risks are and damn the consequences — but Sophie wasn't my daughter.

After we'd eaten, Lindsay got to his feet and said, 'Sophie, my girl. Come with me. There's something I have to show you.' He glanced over at me and winked. 'You come too, Marty.'

He led us out through the back garden of the farm house, whistling loudly. There was a rustle of bushes and out popped a Kelpie.

Lindsay turned to me. 'This is Bess. She's the daughter of one of the best trial dogs I've ever had.'

Bess was a truly striking dog. Her eyes were bright green and she had an unusual silvery-grey coat. She was lying in tightly coiled readiness, trembling all over because she was so keen to get out there and work. Yet her body was glued obediently to the ground, awaiting her master's command, her mesmerising green eyes nailed to Lindsay's.

'Magnificent dog,' I said in appreciation. 'You've trained her brilliantly.'

Lindsay chuckled. 'You know, that's the funny thing. I barely had to train young Bess at all. She's just like her father and her grandmother before her. They just loved herding sheep — all great trial champions do. But Bess is even better — she's like the Leonardo da Vinci of sheep herding.'

He walked to the garden gate and opened it. Before us spread the smooth, rolling hills of sheep country.

Lindsay turned to Bess. 'You know what to do, love. Go bring me those three sheep over there.'

We watched as she silently streaked off towards the target sheep on the far hill. Then she reached them and her true artistry was revealed.

I've seen some fantastic sheep dogs in my time but Bess truly was the Leonardo da Vinci of sheep herding, as Lindsay had said. She was a joy and an inspiration to watch. It was a virtuoso performance.

I turned to congratulate Lindsay, but he was leaning towards Sophie, his arm lovingly around her shoulders.

'Young Bess is like you, love,' he said. 'She's just passionate about her job. Can you imagine taking Bess away from her sheep and sticking her in a small boxed-in backyard in suburbia? Are you picturing it, darling? Sure, she'd be alive and she'd do whatever she was told to do — but her spirit would shrivel up inside her and die.'

'What are you saying, Dad?'

'Don't — whatever you do — *don't* give up this career you feel so deeply and passionately about, Sophie. I truly believe you'll be absolutely miserable doing anything else. Keep at it. Work out a way of showing the world your talent. I just think that once you get your foot in the door, you'll get the chance to rocket ahead like Bess over there.'

I felt like cheering but stayed quiet. This was a special moment between a father and daughter and I could feel the love they had for each other.

Two years later, I heard that Lindsay's advice had paid off for Sophie. Inspired by her father and Bess, Sophie had finally got her job in the film industry. Every time I hear from Lindsay, Sophie seems to be getting another promotion. I haven't seen Sophie since that day on the hill side with her father and Bess — but she must be glad her dad urged her to stick to a career she loved so she could excel in it.

My belief has always been never stop pursuing your dream career. Quite simply, chase your passion. Don't accept a work environment or career you hate. Otherwise you'll be like Bess if she'd been taken away from her hills and sheep and boxed up in a suburban backyard: frustrated, miserable, with your spirit slowly shrivelling up.

Try thinking outside the box

What kind of thinker are you at work? Do you simply repeat ideas you've been taught or told or do you naturally think adventurously?

I believe I'm a very innovative thinker — perhaps because I've lived a bit of an adventurous life. If you suspect your ideas are getting stale and boring, try shaking up your life for a while and watch how your ideas start exciting you and others again.

Gina had a job as a high school art teacher when I met her and she'd decided to move overseas. She called me in to help her rescue dog, Pongo, be adopted by his enthusiastic new owners. Pongo was a huge, black standard Poodle. We took the dog out for a walk to see if he needed to be taught any manners before he went to his new home.

It was hilarious watching everyone's reaction at the park when Pongo bounced onto centre stage. He didn't have the usual fancy Poodle haircut happening — his coat was clean and groomed but just left natural. This meant he was like a giant black curly lamb bouncing around the open park. Everyone just stood still as he bounced into sight, staring at him in wonder.

'What on *earth* is that thing?' we overheard people saying in amazement. 'Is it a dog — or an Alpaca — or a Shetland pony?'

I wiped the tears of laughter from my eyes. 'That dog is just an adventure to watch,' I said.

'Do you know what? Pongo's actually the inspiration behind this huge change in my life,' Gina said proudly.

'Really?' I asked.

'I mean look at him,' she said. 'Wherever he goes he just draws all the attention to him. It's not just his mesmerising looks, it's also all that wonderful, bouncing, optimistic energy he has. No one here in this park has a fraction of the buoyant liveliness that Pongo has.

'Do you know how Pongo changed me? One day I caught myself hauling yet another cardboard box out of my car in the staff car park at school and it was full of artworks that I hadn't created myself. As if in slow motion, I saw all the students and teachers tramp past me with gloomy, dull expressions as they obeyed the school bell and moved to their next class, and I thought, Hell! My dog has a more exciting life than I do!'

She looked at Pongo bouncing around the park now. 'I guess that moment in my school car park was my own personal epiphany. I knew I had to decide right there and then whether I was going to stay in this horribly safe box I'd put myself in, or whether I was going to haul myself out — and escape!'

'Wow!' I said.

'I knew my art was never going to take off here while I was still teaching,' she said.

'So what did you decide to do?' I asked.

'I decided on the spot to buy myself a ticket to Barcelona. I've found a job teaching English over there so I can support myself. Now I plan on pursuing my art in Barcelona as I've always dreamed of doing.'

'Pongo sure helped you jump out of your boring box, didn't he?'

'I know,' she said. 'He's such a gorgeous, inspirational character. I'm ecstatic that I found him such lovely new owners. They adore him.'

'And now you're going to move to a really exciting part of the world,' I said, feeling a bit envious. I love Barcelona.

'Even more importantly, I'm finally getting the chance to come up with much more exciting art!' she said. Her positive energy was just as infectious as Pongo's.

We both looked at the happy-go-lucky Poodle. He looked like a cartoon character bouncing around the park gleefully; the sort of dog that any adventure might happen to. No wonder he'd inspired lucky Gina to completely transform her life. He was the sort of dog who'd get anyone thinking outside the box.

If you need to start thinking outside the box, take your dog to its favourite place to play. Watch the way your dog makes every moment a fun adventure. Be inspired by your dog's natural sense of adventure to think — and live — differently.

You may be good at your job — but there's still a lot you don't know

The day you stop learning is the day you stop living. I truly believe this.

One of the most frustrating things for me is coming across a professional who may be great at his or her job but who never listens to anyone else's ideas. My habit is to suck up all new ideas like a vacuum cleaner — from whatever source — and embrace all that new information. Absorb it, think about it and use it, not only to advance your own career but to come up with ideas that everyone in the world can use.

Anthony, a website designer I knew, got the opportunity to learn this lesson from his dogs, a mongrel called Zeke and an Afghan called Otto.

Anthony was extremely good at his job as a website designer, and he knew it. His work was much sought after, he was raking in the money and his prospects for further promotion looked good. However, he had one very bad habit: Anthony never listened to anyone else's ideas. As he saw it, he was the best in the business and he didn't need to listen to anyone else's ideas.

Interestingly enough, Anthony married another web designer, Natalie, who worked at a different firm. Natalie was the exact opposite of Anthony. She was also great at her job and was rapidly being promoted through the ranks at her company. She never stopped asking other people to give an opinion about her work as it progressed. 'What do you think of this idea?' she asked everyone from the mail courier to the lady who delivered the deli sandwiches. 'Can you please give me your opinion? Do you prefer this version or that version?'

One day Anthony was presenting his latest big web design to the marketing director of a large corporation. The director looked at his work with narrowed eyes. 'I'm not sure about it,' she said at last. 'There's something wrong, something about the overall *atmosphere* of the site. Perhaps ...' She gave him a list of alternative ideas and suggestions.

Anthony, in his usual fashion, argued with all of them. 'No, I think you'll find I'm the professional here. I've been in this industry twenty-five years and I'm very good at what I do.'

In the end, Anthony wouldn't budge, so he lost the lucrative account. He got a roasting from his immediate boss and was warned not to let his ego interfere again. Anthony went back to his office fuming.

He arrived home that evening to find his wife and I discussing how to sort out the arguments between their rescue dogs. They already had an eight-year-old mongrel called Zeke and had just adopted a pure-bred Afghan called Otto. The adoption wasn't going too smoothly, so they'd called me in to help.

'The problem is this, Martin,' said Natalie. 'Just look at that dog — I've never seen anything like it.'

The three of us stared at the glamorous Afghan. He was sitting still, his nose pointed straight up in the air, and he was frozen in that position like a statue.

'Why on earth is he doing it?' Anthony asked. 'I find it kind of spooky.'

I laughed. 'I'll tell you why. Take a look at your other dog, Zeke.'

The three of us looked at the older mongrel who was staring at Otto in fascination. It was obvious the mongrel had never seen anything like Otto the Afghan before — and especially his weird pose.

'So what are we all doing?'

'Staring at Otto,' said Natalie.

'Exactly,' I said. 'And in the Dog World if you can get everyone watching you all the time you make yourself the Boss because you're dominating everyone's attention. Holding that pose is so unusual you can't help but stare. It's just Otto's ingenious way of dominating everyone.'

'How bizarre,' said Natalie.

We were just discussing a behaviour program to help

Otto from feeling so dominant when Natalie got a call on her cell phone from her boss. She excused herself and left the room. When she returned, she was buzzing with excitement. 'My boss just rang. I've got a new client to whom I have to submit a web design proposal.' She named the corporation — and it was the same account that Anthony had just lost.

'It's a small world,' said Anthony sourly.

Natalie looked at him and frowned. 'No need to blame me, darling. Apparently the marketing director wanted to have more input but you were being difficult so she pulled the account from your firm to mine.'

'The lady was an idiot. I've been in web design for twenty-five years and I'm excellent at my job. She should have listened to my ideas.'

Natalie rolled her eyes. 'She did listen to your ideas. The problem was, darling, that you wouldn't listen to *hers*. You forget — I know what it's like doing a project with you. You have a horrible habit of treating everyone else's ideas as unimportant. My motto is you can always learn new ideas from other people, no matter who they are.'

The dogs caught my attention and I laughed out loud. Anthony and Natalie turned to see what I was laughing at. I nodded at the dogs.

The mongrel was now copying the Afghan. He was sitting with his nose pointing upwards like a statue but instead of sitting still he was swaying slowly from side to side. Now the Afghan was staring at him, mesmerised. Zeke, clever mongrel that he was, had learned a new trick from the newcomer dog and added it to his own repertoire.

This is one of the things I really love about dogs — they'll learn new tricks from absolutely anyone.

'I guess you *can* teach an old dog new tricks,' I said.

Natalie gave Anthony a pointed look. 'Guess there's something in that for everyone, darling — don't you think?'

I never discovered if Anthony really learned his lesson from his two dogs, but I hope you do. Clever lead dogs never assume they know everything. They carefully collect every single little scrap of new information they can from every human and dog they meet. Each scrap of information is carefully stored away and remembered, and it's this total dedication to always learning new things that ultimately gives dogs a great winning edge.

So just because you happen to be great at your job, never assume you can't learn something new from someone else — even a young outsider.

Stop running away from your current problems and fears at work

Are you a person who procrastinates about tackling problems at work? Selina was a lady who suffered for years with her anxieties, saying nothing to her boss about her concerns. Finally, her rescued puppy, Arnie, inspired her to go and see her employer and ask for help.

Selina called me out to help with the puppy she'd adopted from her local rescue dog shelter. Arnie was a pup that had been rescued from a raided puppy factory and after he was nursed back to health by the shelter's volunteers, he was put up for adoption. He was a teacup-size Maltese-Poodle.

'Please, Martin,' she said on the phone, 'can you help me with Arnie? He's just so scared. Nothing I do seems to help.'

I arrived at her house and as I always do with scared dogs, I asked the owner to sit with me and simply pretend the dog didn't exist while we had a conversation. In this way, Arnie would get a chance to get used to me being in the house and relax.

I asked Selina what she did for work.

She told me she'd worked in a large government department for over ten years and that she couldn't believe how much the job had changed in that time. She confided that she was miserable in her job because she felt like an old dinosaur at work. She was becoming very stressed because her computing skills were now letting her down.

The reason I was so interested in hearing Selina talk about her job was because I was picking up a surprising amount of anxiety from her. Puppies rescued from puppy factories are usually so traumatised by their past they need an extremely relaxed, confident owner to help them recover from their deeply ingrained fears. It was obvious from listening to Selina that she was going to have to face up to her anxieties at work if she was going to be able to help Arnie relax.

'Selina, listening to you, it seems as though you really have some fears you have to tackle at work. If you don't, you're going to keep bringing your anxieties home to poor Arnie. You almost sound scared of your young colleagues at work.'

She stared at me, then her shoulders sagged. 'Okay, I'll admit it, those damned young kids at the office do scare me. They just have such breezy, careless confidence!' She looked down at Arnie, who was now tentatively padding out from behind the couch and into the middle of the lounge room, cautiously sniffing where my footsteps had been.

'I'm like poor Arnie. Guess that's why I picked the poor little mite — he reminds me of me.' She smiled as the pup glanced shyly at us then scuttled back under the couch. 'I'm just as nervous of everything at work these days as that little pup is of this room. The new attitudes, the technology, the new clothes and manners — I feel like the bitter, sour old fossil in the office everyone's laughing at for being such a useless old prehistoric dinosaur.

'Oh Martin — I can't explain how much I've lost my confidence at work these days! Once upon a time I was the well-dressed, smart woman who was the brilliant office star. Now I feel like I'm completely obsolete.'

I leaned across and gave her a reassuring hug. 'Now, Selina, darling, we can't let this state of affairs drag on like this or you're going to be no good for poor Arnie at all. So how do you suggest we fix this?'

'I guess the only thing I can do is go to my manager and ask for help,' she said.

I gestured at Arnie, who was back hiding behind the couch, only the tip of his nose showing.

'Well, there's your alternative if you don't take the big step, Selina,' I said. 'Arnie here will spend the rest of his life hiding anxiously behind your furniture, scared of his own shadow, and you'll spend the rest of your days at the office, hiding behind your gruff manner, snarling and snapping at all those mocking youngsters. The choice is yours — all you need is to have is a bit of courage.'

She looked over at the pup's twitching nose.

'I'll do it for Arnie,' she said decisively. 'If I've got to sort out this issue of being scared at work then I'll do it for him.' She paused. 'And screw those cheeky youngsters — I refuse to be scared of them any more.'

'That's the spirit.'

She rang me a month later. The behaviour program I'd suggested for Arnie was working wonders and he was gaining his confidence quickly.

'Mainly because I'm turning into such a damned confident person,' she said with a laugh. 'You were right, Martin. It was silly staying so scared at work. I went and saw my manager and she booked me into some fast-track skill improvement courses. Even better — the kids at the office have invited me out for drinks Friday night.'

Whether it's to do with work or not, I believe you should learn to tackle your problems and fears swiftly. Don't run away from them. The best solution is to face your problems head on, no matter how powerful they seem. Either you hide in a corner worrying about them or you nail each fear, one by one. It's up to you.

Disconnect from the world for a while

There comes a moment when you simply have to save your sanity and unplug yourself from everything that keeps you connected to your job — especially all that intrusive technology.

So switch off your computer, cell phone, landline, radio and TV. Why? Sometimes we use technology to subconsciously distract ourselves and keep our minds busy when we would be far better off just sitting still and learning to relax. Craig became so ludicrously addicted to all his technological toys that he even slept with his phone on his pillow. His destructive Labrador-cross, Puss, eventually persuaded him that he needed to make some serious changes in his life.

Craig was one of the most successful lawyers in the city. The problem with being so successful, however, was that he constantly had to be on call for his high-flying clients, with the result that he never switched off his cell phone. I met him as a client because he was having problems with his dog.

When I'd asked him on the phone what the problem was, he'd said grimly, 'She's so destructive. God knows why I called her Puss. She should have been called Chomper because all she does is chew everything I own to bloody bits.'

When I arrived at Craig's harbourside mansion, I discovered Craig hadn't been exaggerating. As I walked through the front garden I had to step over chewed cushions, bits and pieces of chewed hose pipe, a chewed garden chair, several palm trees that had been dragged around by their fronds, what looked like the chewed remains of a huge canvas garden umbrella and several very dead towels.

I rang the doorbell and waited.

There was the sound of barking and footsteps, a voice raised in loud admonishments and the patter of excited dog feet. The door opened to reveal a man on his cell phone, eyes raised to the ceiling as he continued telling whoever was on the phone to 'Pull your head in and *listen* to me, you *idiot* — or you're going to find yourself in *prison* serving three years!'

Beside him, the most gorgeous creamy Labrador-cross-Bull Terrier stood looking out at me in sweet curiosity. This must be Puss, I thought. She looked like butter wouldn't melt in her mouth.

Craig gestured for me to enter and follow him, so Puss and I obediently followed him through the mansion to a sweeping terrace that looked out over the magnificent views of Sydney Harbour.

'Well,' Craig said, after cursing rudely at his client and hanging up mid-argument, 'I can't save the miserable skin of that idiot. This time I refuse to come and visit him in prison. He never listens.' He grinned at me. 'Sorry about that. Can't let the clients down — when it's a crisis, it's a crisis.' He said this with a flourish as though he said it often.

I soon discovered it was the mantra he lived by.

I was just about to suggest we discuss Puss and her highly destructive chewing problem when the aria from *Madame Butterfly* floated around us.

'Sorry, I have to take this call. Big client. All my clients have a different ring tone.'

There was another phone conversation filled with swearing, yelling and admonishments from Craig. The call finally ended with Craig bellowing, 'If you sign that goddamn rip-off contract you're a bigger fool than you look!' He snapped the phone shut and looked at me with a smile. 'Now, where were we?'

I leaned forward in my chair ready to start when Bob Dylan started singing out around us at the top of his voice. 'Sorry, got to take this — brand new client.'

I sat back, feeling annoyance curl around inside my stomach, and glanced across at Puss. She was staring like a zombie into the distance.

'Yeah, I'd switch off too if I were you, darling,' I said to her. 'This is pure craziness, isn't it?'

Craig eventually finished the phone call and turned to me with an apologetic grin. 'Sorry about that, but when it's a crisis, it's a crisis. I can't wait to hear what you have to say about Puss and —'

This time Willie Nelson crooned out a love song around us.

I'd had enough. I held up my hand. '*Stop!* If you don't turn off that bloody thing right this second I'm standing up and walking straight out of here.'

Craig gaped at me. Puss looked from me to the still crooning cell phone and back at her owner. Craig's hands twitched a little as he switched off the phone.

'There, that's better,' I said. 'Now we can hear ourselves *think*. Well? Are you going to sit down and join Puss and I?'

Craig slowly sat. 'You're not like any dog trainer I've ever met,' he said.

'That's because I'm not a dog trainer — I'm a dog communicator,' I said grimly. 'And my job is to help people *communicate* better with their dogs. As far as I can see, Craig, the only thing you bother communicating with around here is that bloody cell phone of yours.'

'It's essential for my job. If my clients can't reach me they —'

I held up my hand to stop him. 'Look, I'm not going to sugar-coat this. You're obviously *addicted* to that cell phone.'

He stared at me blankly.

'Look at you right now,' I said. 'Your hands are twitching like any junkie who's not getting a fix. You're dying to check who called a moment ago. It's driving you crazy not using it. Don't you ever turn the damned thing off at all?'

'I sleep with it on my pillow,' he admitted. 'I never switch it off, even at night.'

I gently slid my hand over Puss's silky head and ears. 'This poor dog feels totally alone in this big house. No wonder she's trying to distract herself by chewing everything in sight. She's completely stressed and that chewing is the only way she can rid herself of all the tension building up inside her. You might spend time here when you're not at the office, but you're not really here — you're just on the phone talking shop all the time. Darling Puss needs someone to spend time with her. Communicating. Bonding. Caring.'

'Okay,' said Craig sulkily. 'I can do that.'

'Yeah?' I said. 'Well, I don't believe you. Like any addict, you're just going to lie to me and your dog and yourself and when I leave you'll just be back on that phone again and poor Puss will be chewing her heart out again.'

I stood up. 'I'm going now. Call me when you're ready to get serious about helping this sweetheart of a dog. By the way — you do know if you keep living this sort of crazy life you're going to end up killing yourself. It's a completely destructive way to live. You're worrying about Puss destroying your possessions — but I suggest you start worrying about how your stupid cell phone is going to destroy your health. As long as it's switched on, you're not getting a chance to switch off from your job. Call me when you're ready to talk properly about your dog,' I said over my shoulder as I walked away.

Craig called me three weeks later, a changed man. Since I'd last seen him, he'd trained his clients to call him between set hours only. The new rule he had was once inside his front door, his phone got switched off. Both he and Puss were much happier after they completed the behaviour program I suggested. Puss stopped chewing everything in sight. Craig sat on his terrace and listened to the music in his vast CD collection, instead of the personalised ring tones of difficult clients.

If you're addicted to your cell phone do something about it before you go crazy. You'll be surprised at how relaxing the world can be once you switch off all your office technology.

Do you quit as soon as things get difficult?

If you're in the habit of quitting a task as soon as things get difficult, maybe you'll be inspired to change when you hear Evan's story. He learned just how determined he could be when he desperately wanted to save a Saint Bernard called Clancy.

I met Evan when I called him out to my farmhouse to make some much needed repairs. My roof needed mending.

A few windows wouldn't close properly. Some parts of the guttering were sagging. The chimney stack was leaking. A few wooden railings were missing from the verandah. What can I say? The house is nearly a hundred years old and it has a few things — well, let's face it — quite a lot wrong with it. My wife, Lee, was nearly dancing around in excitement at the thought of a handyman finally fixing all those annoying problems around the house.

Evan arrived and got straight into Lee's job list. The railings were smartly nailed back on, one by one. The guttering was fixed. Then the pace of work slowed considerably.

'Go and see what's wrong,' Lee hissed in desperation after Evan had pulled off a section of the roof and then did nothing except stare at a tricky section thoughtfully.

I wandered outside, my heart sinking. I recognised that particular expression on his face. He was thinking, 'Oh my God, I have no idea what I'm doing — please send me inspiration right now.'

I sent him a friendly smile. 'Anything I can help with, Evan?'

'No, no. Nothing to worry about. Just thinking things through. Just reached a tricky bit — that's all.'

I walked back inside, deeply worried.

'Well?' hissed Lee.

'All coming along as scheduled,' I said soothingly.

Lee began to look panicky as Evan came and told us he'd just proceed on the windows while he mulled over in his mind how to fix the roof's 'tricky bits', as he called them. He quickly unscrewed the windows from their hinges and laid them out on the grass, then started confidently dismantling part of the wooden window frames. I winced as I saw some fairly important bits of wood crumble in his fingers. Then that same thoughtful look entered his eyes and he went ominously still and silent again.

'Does he even know what he's doing?' hissed Lee, peering furtively through another window at him.

Obviously not, I thought grimly. But no need to hear Lee's nagging any more than necessary. 'I'm sure he does, darling. He's a professional handyman and he was recommended to us.'

The next time I glanced out the window, Evan was pulling the metal cylinder of a chimney stack apart and the pieces were arranged in a neat row across the grass — right next to the neat row of window pieces.

Lee was hopping with anger. It was getting darker and a storm was rolling in from the Border Ranges. We were now without parts of the roof. There was a gap where a line of windows should be. And there was a hole where once our chimney stack had pierced the roof.

'Sorry about that,' said a sheepish Evan. 'Things got a bit tricky with some of the jobs. I'll come and fix them tomorrow.'

'I'll get a tarp,' I suggested and left Lee to deal with Evan.

'That man!' fumed Lee later as rain and wind poured through the house. 'He's hopeless! He just gives up as soon as things get slightly difficult — or *tricky*.'

The next day as gale winds blew, Evan rang up to say he'd caught a bit of a cold and would be out of action for awhile.

Some months later I was surprised to hear back from him.

'You've got to help me,' he said. 'I've been given a rescued dog — it's a Saint Bernard called Clancy. His owners couldn't handle him — he's just so strong and he pulls like the devil on the leash.'

'Oh?' I asked. My heart sank. Stopping a big, strong dog from pulling on the leash takes a lot of determination and Evan wasn't exactly the most determined guy in the world.

'I got Clancy off death row at the local dog pound and I'm his last chance. If I can't teach him to walk okay on the leash, he's going to have to be euthanised. Will you help me Martin?'

I agreed, but my heart sank even further. The thought of Evan ever finishing a task this difficult seemed miraculous.

I went around to his house and showed him how to manage Clancy on a leash.

'Now you won't get success straightaway — you've got to be persistent and stick to the behaviour program I gave you,' I reminded him. 'Just don't give up!'

I wondered if Clancy was going to make it, but I have to admit, I didn't have high hopes.

Three weeks later Evan phoned me and there was a new note of pride in his voice. 'I actually did it, Martin. I've now trained Clancy not to pull on the leash at all.' He laughed. 'I did as you said with Clancy and didn't give up, no matter how difficult it got.'

Amazed, I congratulated him.

'First time I've ever seen a job right through to the end,' he said with a chuckle. 'Young Clancy walks perfectly on the leash now. Gentle as a lamb he is.'

'Good for you, Evan,' I said, impressed. Clancy had been a difficult dog to walk on the leash and I knew he would have had one hell of a job getting this big, strong, stubborn dog to give in and stop pulling.

'You know,' said Evan, 'teaching Clancy really forced me to find the right attitude to get the job done. I sure had to dig deep — but I eventually found the right attitude.'

I agree with Evan. In my experience, the right attitude is the only thing that helps you complete a really difficult job. Perseverance, stubbornness — and having a strong motivation to succeed. These three things make for a great attitude. Lucky for Clancy, Evan dug deep inside himself to finally find the right attitude to finish a task.

Do you work for success like a drudge?

Do we have to work like a drudge if we want a successful life? Personally, I prefer how dogs play their way to success.

This story is about a hard-working lady called Kate whose two dogs inspired her to learn a more playful attitude to work.

I met Kate while she was playing with her pair of Papillons at an inner-city park. Papillons, if you're wondering, are those wonderfully eye-catching little dogs with the big ears that stick up like butterfly wings on either side of their head. Everyone in the park was watching Kate and her two little dogs because they were so brilliant at playing catch together.

Incredibly alert and fit, each dog was superb at waiting, poised for Kate to fling special soft leather balls for them to catch. She flung these balls from a specially designed long-handled plastic scoop. As the balls flew along the ground, bouncing high, each little dog would take turns to leap like a ballet dancer up in the air, catch the ball on the bounce in their mouth and race back to Kate at top speed with it. The three of them had obviously played this game many times before, and a small crowd gathered to watch.

I walked over and fell into easy conversation with Kate.

'These dogs are exceptional at playing this game,' I said.

Kate turned to me and laughed, still panting slightly. 'Oh, this is definitely their favourite game. Meet Lily and Daisy.'

'Isn't it amazing how dogs learn to become brilliant at doing something simply by playing,' I said as both dogs danced eagerly around us, waiting for the ball to be thrown again.

'Tell me about it — if only I felt like this when I'm at work. My job is well paid, but it's pure drudgery.'

I thought of the project I was working on which was rapidly turning into drudgery too. Meanwhile, Lily and Daisy were leaping around us, higher and higher, grins all over their faces, eager for their game to begin again.

'They certainly consider this game to be their job. Even though they play it so enthusiastically, there's an underlying seriousness about it. Every day they can't wait to get out here in the park and round up those cheeky balls.'

'Aren't dogs lucky?' I said. 'They're certainly not stupid enough to work like drudges like us humans. If dogs get bored of doing a task they simply stop. Must be a human thing to make learning and working as boring as possible.'

'Heavens, I always thought being a contract lawyer would be my dream job, but every day is just more hard slog.'

'I know,' I said, 'let's go back to work with a dog's attitude. The next time we walk into our job, let's have the attitude that we're going to play our way through the job rather than drearily slog our way through it.'

'Okay,' she said with a surprised laugh. 'My job could certainly do with some fun. I see the older lawyers around the office — they're like grim-faced zombies.'

'So?' I asked. 'What do you think? Go to work tomorrow and try and play our way through it?'

'Sure,' she said.

We left the park, Kate with Lily and Daisy and me with a mind racing with ideas of how to make the next day at work more playful.

'Well?' It was Kate on the phone the following evening. 'How did you do? Did you play or slog?'

'Played like a dog,' I said. 'And by your cheerful voice, I can tell you did too.'

'I did,' she said. 'Listen to this for inspiration. I organised our usual boring office meeting to take place out in the courtyard so we could catch some sun — and we got far more interesting ideas than usual. At lunch I put a sitcom up on the conference screen for everyone to relax in front of for half an hour. Even better, I wore a T-shirt under my usual blazer that read, "PLAY HARD — WORK HARD". It got everyone talking and laughing. I actually had a really fun day at work today for once — and so did everyone else. My boss was impressed by the way we all perked up. How about you?'

'Well, I turned a teaching lecture I was supposed to give into a demonstration. I actually got the vet students to get down on their hands and knees and pretend they were misbehaving dogs so I could go around showing them how to fix the problem behaviours. The students loved it.'

'That was a great idea.'

'Kate, wherever I can I'm going to be like a dog and play my way through work.'

'You betcha,' said Kate. 'It's time to introduce more play into my life.'

As I hung up the phone I thought of little Lily and Daisy who played their way through life yet were so superb at their job of fetching the ball.

Perhaps it's up to all of us to wipe drudgery out of the work place?

Choose your battles in life — especially at the office

Learn to choose your battles. At work decide which issues are worth fighting for and which aren't worth wasting your energy on. As any dog can tell you, if you find yourself with a fight on your hands then strategy is very important.

Bernadette called me out for a consultation because she was having problems with her two dogs, an older Cairn Terrier called Puck and her younger teenage dog, a Curly Coated Retriever called Jeep. I arrived at her home to find a familiar situation. There was Jeep, a bothersome teenage dog, high on hormones and overflowing with far too much energy. And poor Puck, an exhausted, nerve-stretched older dog doing his best to cope with this annoying young dog he could never escape from.

Bernadette was very frustrated. 'The dogs get on most of the time but a few times a day there's a real scuffle and little Puck just seems to erupt into a fight for no apparent reason. I was wondering if he was going senile or something,' she told me.

'Nope, Puck's not senile,' I said, looking at him. 'He's actually a wise old dog who's simply choosing his battles.' I looked at the workmanlike dog with his coarse, dark grey coat. The dog's sparkly eyes looked up at me from under his shaggy topknot. 'You're a smart little thing, aren't you?' I asked. I turned to Bernadette. 'Let me guess when he erupts into a fight: when visitors arrive, and at dinner time, and when they go to lie down to sleep at night.'

'How on earth did you know that? Those times are *exactly* when Puck explodes into a full attack on poor Jeep.' She fondled Jeep's curl-covered ears reassuringly. 'Poor Jeep isn't doing anything wrong at all except trying to play with Puck and that little bully just goes crazy and attacks him.'

I explained that in reality Puck had every right to stop the younger, pushier Jeep from trying to dominate him all the time. 'The reason Puck explodes those few times a day is because he's wise enough to choose his battles very carefully. If he tried to keep young Jeep here under control all the time he'd soon wear himself out. So he simply chooses the most important battles he has to win each day — and makes damned sure he wins them. That's what those explosive fights are — Puck just making sure he wins the most important battles.'

'Ah,' said Bernadette. 'I get it. Let me guess which are the most important battles that Puck wants to win: who controls dinnertime and the best sleeping spot, and —'

'And who controls the visitors when they come onto your territory,' I finished for her.

'Funnily enough, I might be able to learn something from Puck and apply it to the office politics at work at the moment,' she said.

'We can all learn something from dogs when it comes to dealing with office politics,' I said with a laugh. 'Dogs are even more ambitious than humans, I think.'

'Hmm,' said Bernadette. 'You haven't seen my office. It's like a shark pool. Show any weakness and the young, ambitious sharks start zooming in, nibbling at your authority.'

'Just like Jeep here does to Puck all the time.'

'Worse — at least Jeep is upfront about trying to dominate old Puck. These ambitious young sharks are very sly, they just keep nibbling and nipping around my edges, trying to push me aside and grab my job.'

'Take a page out of wise old Puck's book then — be smart when the youngsters try to overwhelm you with their energy. Simply choose your battles at work, make damn sure the battles are important and make sure you win them!'

Three weeks later I rang Bernadette to see how the dogs were progressing.

'Excellent, Martin,' she said. 'Puck and Jeep aren't having any more fights now. Thank you — it's wonderful having a peaceful home again without any unnecessary dog politics. Listen — speaking of politics, I have to tell you what's happened at my office since I last saw you, because it'll make you laugh.'

'Oh? So you decided to use some of Puck's strategies against those young sharks?' I asked, settling back into my chair in enjoyment.

'I sure did,' she said smugly. 'I picked my battle *very* carefully. We had to give a big presentation at work and I didn't waste any energy arguing beforehand with the sharks, I just waited until the middle of the presentation to give everyone my ideas and argued my case with an intense energy no one was expecting. I surprised everyone with my unexpected attack. The executive board was most impressed with my arguments and I got the promotion I wanted.'

'Congratulations!'

'I wish you could have seen the young sharks' faces after the presentation.'

'Dumbfounded, I bet,' I said, 'after you finished *Pucking* with them.'

If you're like Bernadette and feeling the ambitious young sharks nibbling at your heels in the office, why don't you borrow the same clever strategy used by wise old dogs like Puck to help maintain your authority and higher position?

Just make sure you choose the right battle to Puck them.

Learn to confuse your enemies like a wise dog

Next time you're in a meeting and you know your office enemies are snapping and snarling at your heels, trying to make your ideas seem stupid in front of the boss, learn this clever trick from supremely confident dogs: Pretend there isn't a fight situation going on. Why? Because when you start defending yourself, you immediately give away your fight strategy. You also make your enemies feel important. Instead, ignore the competition and focus on impressing your boss with your incredible calm control of the situation and your brilliant ideas.

Whenever I use this winning business strategy myself, I'm always reminded of a very clever little Pug called Clint.

A lady called Nora, who was a volunteer with a dog-rescue organisation, had called me in to help with five big dogs in her care who wouldn't stop arguing among themselves. Nora introduced me to the dogs and I suggested we sit and discuss a behaviour program to stop the fighting.

As we sat down, a perky fawn and black Pug trotted into the room and stopped to survey us. The five big dogs all stood up and started circling the surprisingly calm Pug, sniffing it intently.

'Oh dear,' said Nora. 'I'm always scared this little one's going to get badly attacked by the others, but he never does. It's incredible how he has them all bluffed with his unshakeable confidence.'

I watched in curiosity as the Pug simply assumed the five much larger dogs weren't a threat to him. He yawned sleepily and trotted calmly over to Nora and lay down at her feet. The Pug was so calm and confident in the midst of the other dogs' aggressive energy it was incredible.

'What an amazing dog,' I said. 'What's his name?'

'This is Clint. He isn't supposed to stay here permanently — I promised my husband we wouldn't adopt any of these rescue dogs ourselves — but I can't help being impressed by the little fellow.' She shook her head as she chuckled. 'I've never met such a well-behaved dog. Even when these big dogs try to start a fight and growl and snarl at him, he just pretends he can't see any aggression going on around him and acts very calm and normal. The big dogs end up wandering off in confusion, leaving him alone.'

'That's one hell of a confident little cookie,' I said. 'And damned clever too.'

Nora nodded. 'No other dog can fluster him — no matter what they try. Clint just refuses to get scared or fight. He always stays calmly in control of any situation.'

'How on earth are you going to be able to hand him on to someone else to adopt?' I asked.

Nora looked at me and winked. 'Don't worry — I'm working on my husband. Clint's staying.'

I returned a week later and found my anti-fighting program was working a treat. Nora introduced me to her husband, Tony, and we all sat in the living room.

'By the way, Martin,' Nora said. 'Clint's going to be staying. We're adopting him.'

'Excellent,' I said. 'Congratulations.'

Nora went to make us all coffee, leaving me with Tony for company. Curious, I asked him what he thought about having all these strange dogs in the house — especially when they'd been giving Nora so much trouble with their fighting.

Tony puffed out his cheeks and gave me a weary look. 'After the dirty fighting politics I have to deal with at work these days,' he said, 'these rescue dogs are nothing.'

'Oh?' I asked, surprised. 'What do you do for work?'

He rolled his eyes. 'I work in a communications company. In this depressed economic climate it's dog-eat-dog time.' He gestured at the five big dogs. 'I reckon I could now teach these big buggers a thing or two. You wouldn't believe how savage it can get in our monthly meetings nowadays.'

'Why's that?'

'For example — our usual monthly meeting was today. On the surface it looks like a normal office meeting where you're presenting an idea to your boss and you're surrounded by your work colleagues. But these days your work colleagues have become your enemies because none of us want to get sacked. This means we're all madly fighting to impress the boss, trying to weaken our opponents by making all their ideas seem stupid. The monthly meetings have become savage blood baths because if your enemies sense you're weak, they circle in for the kill and rip your ideas to shreds.'

'That's terrible.'

Tony shrugged. 'Tough economic times. Everyone's fighting for survival.'

I looked down at Clint the Pug. An idea came to me. 'Tony? At next month's office meeting, why don't you act more like Clint here?'

Tony sat up straighter. A faintly mischievous smile touched his lips. 'And treat my nasty colleagues just as Clint treats these five big knuckle-headed dogs here?'

'Exactly.'

'So my strategy is to act like Clint and ignore everyone else's hostility. I just keep calmly presenting my ideas to the boss and pretending the others don't even exist. Brilliant.'

'Thanks Clint,' I said.

Nora returned with the coffees and flicked us both a suspicious glance. 'Okay, I recognise that look — what are you two cooking up now?'

We smiled back innocently.

'Nothing, dear,' said Tony.

The following month I got a text message from Tony: *Game plan we called clint: successful. Thanx.*

Don't lose your soul along the way

You certainly meet interesting people when you make the same regular walk along the beach with your dog every day. You see the same people so often that you eventually fall into conversation with them. That's how I met Matt, a man who lost his soul at work, and then found it again through his dog, Lolly.

Matt was forty-three and making his swift way up the corporate ladder at a well-known public relations firm. He loved walking his Labrador, Lolly, every morning along the beach before work. When I first met him he smiled a warm welcome every time I saw him but that smile began to look increasingly worn around the edges. One morning we were in the beach car park and I saw him hesitate, then come over.

'Martin, do you mind if I share some thoughts with you today? I've got something pretty heavy on my mind.'

'Sure,' I said. We fell into step together and headed for the beach. A beautiful dawn was breaking around us.

'I think I'm losing my soul,' he blurted out. 'At work I'm turning into the sort of man I don't like. I make decisions I despise, help people to do truly rotten things to others and get paid a staggering amount of money to do it.'

'If you think you're doing stuff that's bad for your soul your body will let you know,' I said. 'I truly believe that.'

'I'm a believer, don't worry,' he said. 'Lately my stomach's in knots, I've got non-stop headaches, I don't really feel like eating and I'm not sleeping well.'

I glanced across at him. 'Yeah, that sounds like you don't feel good about your job. But only you can decide what you're going to do about it.'

Matt looked around at the beach, the sky, the ocean and down at the grinning, wagging Lolly at his side. 'Whenever I'm here at the beach with Lolly I *know* I'm losing my soul,' he said. 'The trouble is when I'm at work everything just seems normal. That's the nature of the corporate world. It's filled with people who sicken me. Yet I have to keep schmoozing each client as I smile, smile, smile.' He took a deep breath. 'I'll be honest. The most popular drawer in our entire office is the one that's kept stuffed to the brim with headache tablets.'

'Headaches are your body's way of telling you that your job is steadily getting more toxic,' I said.

'Yeah, well, the really big bucks are to be found representing the biggest, baddest clients. You know the sort: tobacco companies, corporations whose products have developed dangerous complications, mining companies, pulping mills shredding ancient forests into paper. The bigger their problem, the more we get paid to sort it out. The only problem, is that inside my head I'm being torn apart. I now represent everything that I'd been brought up by my parents to fight against.'

'So what's stopping you from leaving?' I asked.

'Mortgage. Car loan. Ambition. I mean, this is the lifestyle I always dreamed about having and I've worked damned hard to get it. I've literally invested years of my life to get exactly where I am right now.'

Here was a man truly struggling to retain his soul.

'Only you can decide how you're going to live your life,' I said. 'I think you have to look at yourself in the mirror when you shave every morning — and you have to look Lolly in the eye every evening when you come home. She looks at you with pure adoration. You've earned her trust and love and respect. Trouble is, do you respect yourself these days?'

'Gee — you don't pull your punches, do you, Marty?' he said.

'It's your soul, Matt,' I said. 'Your soul.'

We finished the walk in silence and he drove home to mull over what we'd discussed.

When we next met on the beach walk, he'd obviously had a change of heart.

'Hey, Marty — you know what we were discussing yesterday? Well, forget it. I was just having a soft day. Things must have been getting on top of me at work, I guess.'

'Sure,' I said.

Obviously his soul wasn't winning today. I wondered whether he was going to be able to live without it. We've all met plenty of people in big business who've lost their soul and never go looking for it again.

But only Matt could decide how he was going to live his life.

Three weeks later, Matt jogged up to me on the beach as I was walking my dog and, without warning, wrapped me in a huge bear hug.

'You look happy.' I laughed.

'Happy? I'm ecstatic! I've quit that bloody awful job forever! You'll be happy to know my soul is back — and it's back for good.' Lolly bounced around him happily, barking. Matt's genuine joy was contagious.

I shook his hand. 'Good for you! What happened?'

'Soon after you gave me the tough pep talk, I found myself at my desk at work looking down at the proposed PR campaign I was designing for a giant tobacco company and something just snapped inside me. I thought to myself, I just can't do this job any more. In fact, I felt so ill that I walked straight to the staff bathroom and vomited into the toilet. I guess it was my body's way of finally telling me that my job was getting dangerously toxic for me. I resigned that day.' He tossed a stick for Lolly to fetch. 'I've now got a new job with less money but more ethical clients. I'm so much happier — and I feel far more comfortable in my skin. I enjoy looking around knowing that I'm going to make the world a better place. I feel great!'

'That's because you got your soul back,' I said.

Now Matt looked just as happy and carefree as Lolly.

If you suspect that you're losing your soul at work, take a moment to ask yourself if the material rewards are worth risking your happiness, peace of mind and maybe even your health. Dogs never seem to lose their souls, do they?

Follow your calling

Some of the most impressive people I've met are those who've decided to follow their calling in life. By this I mean they have felt driven to choose a career or a lifestyle that helps to make the world a better place. Striving to make big changes to the world, they usually choose a life of sacrifice, filled with difficult obstacles. However, people I've met who have followed their calling said the same thing: that although plenty of voices advised them to drop their ideas, the only voices that mattered were the small voices inside them. These voices never stopped urging them to use their special talents to make the world a better place.

Wendy followed her calling and in the beginning her only supporter was a Whippet called Snoopy.

Wendy was from a very privileged, wealthy background and had received an excellent, expensive education at one of the best schools in England. She was from a family of surgeons — her father, mother and brother were all very successful and highly thought of within the medical community — and it was expected of her that she'd follow in their footsteps and become a surgeon too. Her marks were extremely high and as she was very driven, getting into a good university to study medicine seemed certain.

However, in her last year of high school, Wendy realised that she actually wanted to be a primary school teacher. Much to her parents' horror, she wanted to follow her calling and teach kids from disadvantaged backgrounds in inner-city London. As you can imagine, her parents were shocked, angry, baffled, frustrated and ultimately confused.

Why did their highly intelligent, talented, beautiful daughter want to throw away her life on such a lost cause?

They cut off her allowance when she chose to study at an excellent teaching university. Wendy simply moved into cheap student digs and got a part-time job at night working in a café. Her family was rude and cold to her, livid with her decision to stick with her teaching career. However, Wendy calmly stayed in contact with them, making regular phone calls and occasionally sending postcards.

But when Wendy actually went and found herself a teaching job in one of the toughest inner-city areas of London, her family was so furious that they cut off all contact with her. This, Wendy told me later, was her darkest hour: the kids were deeply suspicious of her cut-crystal accent; her family had disowned her; and worse, the rest of the teaching staff mocked and were openly hostile to her.

That was what hurt her the most. She'd expected to make plenty of friends among her colleagues so she'd have a support network in a tough, demanding job. She did make a few genuine friends among the staff but there were many aggressively rude and bullying staff members who did everything in their power to make her life at work difficult. The only reason she kept going was because teaching those kids truly was her calling.

As she said to me, 'Sometimes you have to break the rules around you to keep the rules within you. I have no choice. Everything inside me knows I'm a natural-born teacher and that I have a real gift for helping these kids bring out their full learning potential. I know who I am deep inside my core and I'm not going to let others bully me. I'm certainly not a coward when it comes to following my calling.'

She described how she loved that gradual build-up of curiosity in her students, seeing them start to switch on and learn new ideas. She loved gaining their trust and watching her students discover where their talents lay, and the joy of watching their young minds realise that you can actually love learning. As she talked about her job, her eyes would light up and her voice would reveal how passionate she was about helping her students.

However, she admitted that when she got home to her apartment in the evenings she felt a wave of weariness descend over her. Although she felt energised whenever she was around her students, when she was on her own, she felt her spirit weaken. That was when I suggested she get herself a dog. Someone to nurture her for once. A close and loving companion who wouldn't judge her for choosing to follow her calling.

A few days later, Wendy went to Battersea Dog's Home and brought home Snoopy, a beautiful Whippet with a coat striped like a humbug, and loving eyes the colour of dark chocolate.

Once Snoopy entered Wendy's life, things got easier. This sleek little dog was so reassuring and gentle. He had a calm kindness around him that replenished her spirit so she could unwind at night and switch off from her demanding job.

Even better, with Snoopy in her life, she now had the emotional energy to handle any bullying staff member and as she stood up for herself more, the bullying dropped off and was slowly replaced with grudging respect.

Although Wendy was following her calling it was Snoopy who helped her get through the really tough issues.

If you know you're driven to change the world in some way and you have what it takes, then obey that inner voice — follow your calling. But make damn sure you have someone to nurture and care and love you or you're going to burn out along the way. In my opinion, you can't ask for a more nurturing, supportive companion than a dog. With a dog at your side, I believe obstacles just look smaller.

5

What can dogs teach us about relationships?

Dogs, being natural pack animals, are incredibly aware of all the relationship politics going on around them — especially among humans. In fact, I believe dogs are the world's most sensitive barometers, and can instinctively measure human emotions and tensions, telling you instantly whether a human relationship is working or not. Over the years I've seen many people learn how to use the sensitive antennae of their dogs to help them make their relationships healthier, more fulfilling and loving.

Don't let the people closest to you poke holes in your heart

If you're allowing the people closest to you to constantly poke holes in your heart you need to take action. Start valuing yourself enough so you only spend time with people who treat you affectionately and kindly — who make you feel safe.

Nelson was a beautiful greyhound who inspired his owner, Joel, to finally leave the cruel girlfriend who'd enjoyed poking holes in his heart for years.

Joel rang me about a dog problem.

'Hello, Martin, I was wondering if you could come out and help me? My girlfriend, Hillary, has a little Scottish Terrier called Lucky. He doesn't like me and now he's nipping me.'

The moment I walked in their door, I knew I was in a deeply unhappy household. Joel was polite and warm in his greetings to me, but Hillary stood back and watched me with a strange smirk on her face. When I looked into her eyes I saw something you don't see very often — cruelty.

'And this is Lucky,' said Joel as a little Scottish Terrier trotted into the room in a very dominant, self-important way. The dog gave me an aloof look, then headed straight for Hillary. Lucky immediately leapt up to join her on the couch.

I watched with interest as she bent down and cooed: 'There, there now, my poor little darling man. Silly Joel's feeling all upset because he thinks I spoil you — but you can't help loving me so much, can you, darling man?'

I gave the woman a thoughtful look but said nothing. Her tone was cruel — and her words were obviously designed to hurt and belittle Joel. I glanced at Joel. He was watching the pair a little sadly. Then he turned to me and invited me to sit down too.

In the next half-hour, while we discussed the problem, I watched a very malicious woman delight in using that poor little dog as a weapon to hurt her boyfriend as much as she could. In every gesture and word she emphasised how much she enjoyed deliberately withholding her love from her boyfriend. Her vindictiveness made me feel sick to the stomach.

Meanwhile, Lucky was enjoying his dominance over Joel too. He nipped Joel at every possible chance.

Whenever her dog did this, Hillary burst into peals of loud laughter. 'Oh dear, Joel — it doesn't look like darling little Lucky likes you very much today, does he?'

In the end, it was obvious Hillary had no intention of following any part of the behaviour program I was suggesting, so I called a halt to the consultation.

As Joel walked me back out to my car, I stopped on the driveway and turned to him. 'Hell, man,' I said. 'You've got to get out of this nightmare of a relationship. That woman isn't going to stop poking holes in your heart until she's satisfied you've got nothing left to poke at.'

'I hear what you're saying, Martin. Believe me, this situation only crept up on me slowly. Hillary wasn't always like this. Since she's got Lucky, she's become really nasty.'

'Joel, this home situation is completely toxic. You're worth more than this.'

'I know that inside my head,' he said. 'But I guess you start to believe the bad things people say about you after a while.'

Joel had had so many bits of his self-worth chipped off him that he'd become a husk of a man.

'My advice, Joel? Get yourself a dog,' I said, getting into my car. 'Then you'll remember what real affection and compassion are again.'

Nine months later I ran into Joel at the local markets. He'd changed so much, it actually took me a few moments to recognise him.

'It's me, Martin — Joel. You came out to help me with a dog called Lucky.'

Gone was the haunted-looking, insecure husk of a man I remembered who'd almost slunk around like a kicked puppy. Now a vibrant, energy-filled man stood before me with a face that was unmistakably happy. The pieces fell into place as I recognised him. I glanced down at the sleek, beautiful blue Greyhound on a leash at his side.

'What a magnificent dog,' I said in appreciation.

'This is Nelson,' Joel said. 'He's from my local Greyhound rescue group. He changed my life around.'

'Thank God,' I said. 'You were living deep in a nightmare. I'm sure Lucky wasn't happy about you getting a new dog.'

'No, Lucky and Hillary definitely had their noses pushed out of joint when Nelson came to live with me.'

'You seem like such a different man,' I said. 'What happened to you?'

'You were right when you said I should get myself a dog,' he said with a laugh. 'After a week with Nelson in my life, I quickly remembered what real love felt like again.'

I nodded. 'I believe an affectionate dog quickly unravels all the bad things people do to you.'

'That's for sure. After I got Nelson, I started believing in myself again. I left Hillary and started dating. I want you to meet my darling Lauren. Here she is.' He introduced his new girlfriend to me.

Looking at her, I felt my eyes widen in surprise. No woman could have been more different from Hillary. Lauren was pretty in a warm way, her eyes shone with kindness and happiness. There wasn't a whiff of cruelty about her.

'I'm so happy to meet you,' I said, shaking her hand.

Joel's heart was definitely going to be safe in the care of Nelson and Lauren.

If you're in a situation where the person closest to you is deliberately poking holes in your heart, get out as fast as your feet can carry you. Nobody deserves to be treated like that. If you're feeling unlovable after such an ordeal, consider getting a kind, gentle-natured dog because when a dog loves you, the holes in your heart heal.

Make your home your private sanctuary

Is your home a peaceful, nurturing place to return to every evening after work? If not, why not? In your home you have every right to feel respected and cared for by those who are closest to you. After all, home is where you finally get a chance to safely lower all your personal barriers and be nurtured.

Helen learned through her three rescue dogs to finally insist that everyone in her family respect her sacred home space.

The evening phone call from Helen was distressed: 'Oh God! I can't handle it any more! Can you come and help me with these bloody rescue dogs of mine — they're driving me crazy the way they act like maniacs around my house!'

Helen was a single parent with three teenage boys and three rescue dogs and she worked in a busy medical practice as a receptionist during the day. As she opened the door to me, a flood of dogs poured out around my legs in a noisy, barking mass.

'Oh God!' Helen looked at me, then at the dogs swirling around us. Her face was lined with exhaustion and helpless frustration. 'Sorry, but the bloody wretches are running totally out of control at the moment.'

I soon relaxed the three dogs — a Border Collie, a Jack Russell and a brindle Staffy — by giving them natural calming signals. As expected, the dogs started relaxing around us and we walked to the living room in a much calmer manner.

Helen stared at them in amazement. 'Are these my dogs? I've never seen them this calm before — especially around visitors.'

I suggested we sit down and I'd take her through a behaviour program to teach the dogs more respectful manners. We were sitting, talking, and the dogs had calmly settled in a quiet circle around us when raucous male voices came crashing through the house. The dogs erupted into noisy barking and ran around in a frenzied mass then surged out in a furry wave to the front door.

I looked at Helen.

'My teenage sons,' she said. 'This is the time of the day I dread the most. I come home exhausted from work, wanting to relax peacefully, and the boys come home, crashing around like cavemen.'

The noise got closer, with the dogs whipping themselves up into even more of a frenzy. There were loud jeers. Something that sounded like a football was kicked against a wall to be greeted with roars of approval and someone groaning.

I glanced across at Helen. Her face was turned to the ceiling, her eyes closed, one hand massaging her forehead.

Within seconds, a heaving, wrestling mass of teenagers spilled through the door, surrounded by the dogs barking their heads off. A half-hearted punch-up started among the teenagers and the dogs found an even louder volume of barking.

I'd had enough. The pure animal within me reacted and before I knew it I was straight among the boys, jamming my nose right in the face of the tallest kid. I glared at him, eye to eye.

The mass of boys faltered to a standstill and disentangled themselves. So did the dogs.

'Who are you?' one of the boys asked.

'I want to know why the hell you lot are making such a riot inside your mother's home when you know how tired she is,' I said calmly.

Three boys glared at me sulkily.

Helen started clapping. 'Thank you, Martin. Some blessed peace at last.'

I asked the boys to sit with us. 'Your poor mum is left to deal with the dogs every time you trigger them like that.'

There was silence.

'If you keep up this out-of-control behaviour, you risk the dogs being sent back to the rescue shelter. The neighbours are complaining and your poor mum's nerves can't take it any more.'

'You can say that again,' muttered Helen.

'From now on, you three boys are going to treat the inside of this house with respect. Do you know why?'

They shook their heads, but their eyes never left mine.

'Because if you're not respecting your mum's home, then you're not respecting her either.' I paused to give them time to absorb that and turned to Helen. 'Darling, you have to start demanding that your home is treated as your safe sanctuary, because if you don't start unwinding at night, you're going to end up shredding your nerves to pieces.'

'I'll try, Martin,' she said. 'Some evenings I'm pretty exhausted though.'

I turned to Helen's sons. 'Well, boys, it's up to you to make this work, because if you don't want these three dogs to be dumped back to the rescue shelter then you're just going to have to grow up. You all need to start acting calmly and quietly around the house. Keep all that teenage roughhousing for outside at the park and school.'

The boys looked sheepishly at me, then their mother.

'Sorry,' said the eldest son. 'We're so sorry, Mum. We really respect you for all the things you do for us.'

'And we'll make sure the dogs are quieter too,' said the middle son.

The youngest son got up and gave her a heartfelt hug. 'Don't worry — we won't let you go nutso, Mum.'

I smiled to myself. I had a feeling things were going to be a whole lot quieter around here in future.

From now on, do whatever is necessary to make sure your home is a safe, nurturing sanctuary. Not only is your happiness at stake — so is your sanity.

Stop chasing after someone who doesn't want to be caught

Do you have a bad habit of chasing after people who don't want to be caught? Jackie was finally convinced to stop chasing after her ex-lover by following her elderly dog Reggie's example.

I was living in the inner-city and my friend and neighbour Jackie used to drop in once a week. Unfortunately her topic of conversation always slid back onto the subject of her ex-lover. 'Martin? You won't *believe* what Rick said to me today — he was such a goddamn pig!'

I wasn't her only friend to grit their teeth at the mention of Rick.

I stood aside and smiled down at Reggie as he followed his mistress stiffly through the door. Reggie was Jackie's elderly Labrador-cross-Kelpie and, in my opinion, he was worth a thousand Ricks. He was a real old gentleman of a dog. His muzzle and paws were starting to go white. His hips were a bit sore but he still somehow managed to lumber after Jackie as she darted around the neighbourhood. Unlike Rick, Reggie was always welcome through my door.

'Want to share some of my pasta?' I asked, trying to steer Jackie off her favourite subject.

'No. Far too fattening — and Rick said I was putting on a bit of weight lately.' She plunked herself down on one of my kitchen chairs. 'Now shut up and listen to what Rick said to me today, the rude bastard.'

I sat down and started eating. I kept glancing at this lady sitting across the table from me who'd been chasing after her ex-lover for nearly eight months. Reggie settled down on the rug and let out a loud sigh. He knew that when Jackie was in this sort of mood she could rant and rave and complain about Rick for hours.

There was a knock at the door and I opened it to find my friend Tom with his teenage Mastiff, Jungle. The Mastiff took one look at Reggie, barked in delight and bounded inside on big ridiculous paws the size of dinner plates.

Tom smiled at me and came in too. 'Sorry, Martin, but you're one of the few people who doesn't mind having Jungle as a visitor.'

Reggie glared at Jungle and growled low in his throat. I looked at the elderly dog in sympathy. He simply didn't have the energy, strength or patience to deal with an over-exuberant teenager like Jungle these days. Reggie got up laboriously, wandered over to my couch and hauled himself up on it. Jungle bounding happily after him, got his nose sharply bitten for his troubles. He yelped in shock. Cranky at being disturbed yet again, Reggie slid off the couch and walked stiffly off to my bedroom.

Jackie got up to sort them out, but I stopped her.

'You should watch this,' I said, nodding at the dogs. 'Reggie could teach you a thing or two about the way you keep wasting your time chasing after Rick in such a pointless way.'

Tom rolled his eyes. 'Please, Martin, I'm not in the mood for your dog guru stuff tonight. Just pass the pasta.'

'Shut up,' I said mildly. I looked at Jackie. 'Come on. You're so much like Jungle when you chase after Rick — and just like Jungle, you keep following after someone who doesn't want to know you at this point in their life.'

We watched as Jungle bounced across the room and disappeared after poor Reggie through my bedroom door.

A loud yelp went through the air.

'Am I really that pathetic?' Jackie asked quietly.

There was another loud yelp from the bedroom.

'Yes,' said Tom and I in unison.

'But we like you anyway,' I said, hugging her.

'Except when you mention Rick,' said Tom. 'I hate that name now. Please don't ever mention that slimy bugger's name again.'

Reggie waddled out of my bedroom and disappeared under the table. He bumped us gently with his nose to let us know he was there.

Jackie looked at me sadly. 'I really love Rick, you know.'

I looked at her. 'That's good — but it's not enough, is it? As Reggie just showed Jungle, if someone's not interested in you then all you can do is accept it. You can't waste your life chasing after someone who doesn't want to be caught. You'll just keep getting hurt for nothing.'

Jackie grimaced and reached down to stroke Reggie's ears. 'God, I hate it when you're right.' She took a deep breath. 'Okay, this is it. I guess this is finally my ultimate goodbye-lover moment. Farewell, Rick — forever.'

Reggie licked her hand gently as though to remind her she wasn't alone.

If you're chasing after someone who doesn't want to be caught, accept it. You can't force anyone to love you. If your ex-lover is running away, then they're trying to tell you something but you're not listening.

Stop tolerating other people's negativity

Every time you put up with someone being negative around you, a little bit more of your precious energy bleeds away. Instead, you should be investing that energy in yourself. At the end of the day, you're the only person who can stop other people's poisonous words and actions from invading your heart and mind.

Jamilla didn't know how to stop others from belittling her in small ways. Fortunately, one rescue dog, Joe, finally persuaded her to reset her boundaries and stop allowing other people's negativity to touch her.

I met Jamilla, a truly sweet lady, at a dog-rescue shelter. She was an exceptionally good volunteer because she was endlessly patient when retraining problem dogs — especially dogs who hauled you along on the leash. However, the way she allowed people to put her down with their small, negative comments used to drive me crazy.

For instance, one day I was at the shelter working with a big, headstrong Rhodesian Ridgeback and Jamilla was helping me. Another volunteer arrived and without warning said, 'Gee, Jamilla, no offence, darling, but I'm not sure that new hairstyle quite suits you.'

Sensing a bully, I stopped working the dog and looked up. Sure enough, the 'helpful' friend was standing, hand on hip, head slightly tilted to one side, examining Jamilla's hair thoughtfully. I waited to hear how Jamilla would respond. *Come on — put that rude lady in her place*, I urged her silently.

But Jamilla absorbed the criticism with a weak smile, saying, 'Oh really? I thought it looked nice.'

Rude Lady just smirked a little and wandered off.

Later, I saw Jamilla patting and fussing at her hair as she winced. It was obvious Rude Lady's barb had hit a soft spot and poor Jamilla was feeling yet another little bit of her self-worth bleed away. I decided I had to say something.

'Jamilla, you've got to stop being so thin-skinned,' I said on my last day at the shelter.

'I know I do, Martin,' she said. 'Although I pretend not to care when people say negative things to me, I do care. There's been many a day I've walked out of here trying not to cry. Sometimes I lay awake all night dwelling on the things someone's said to me that day.'

I was in the middle of working a sparky Australian Terrier and in that moment, a sudden idea came to me. I held out the little dog's leash to her. 'It's about time you toughened up, Jamilla, and stopped allowing people to dump all their negative comments on you.'

'Yes?' she said in an uncertain voice. 'And how's this beautiful little dog going to help me do that?'

'This is Joe and I think he's such a character he'll teach you to stand up for yourself if anyone tries to say something negative and hurtful to you.'

'Oh? What's his problem?'

'Joe pulls like a steam train on the leash. No one can walk him without him trying his hardest to choke himself. Watch this.'

I took a few steps forward and Joe rushed ahead, instantly pulling as hard as he could on the leash, choking and wheezing until Jamilla cried out in distress. I stopped walking and Joe finally settled down, coughing and panting heavily.

'Trouble is, if we can't get him walking politely on the leash he's going to be euthanised. He's got a week or he gets the green needle.'

Jamilla leaned over and patted his head in horror. 'Oh, the poor little thing. He's so gorgeous.'

I decided to pluck at her kind heartstrings a bit more.

'Ah well,' I said, 'you do realise everyone's going to try to ridicule you for trying to save this dog, don't you? Quite a few people are saying Joe should be euthanised now — so be ready for plenty of negative comments heading your way this week.'

Jamilla's chin shot up. 'Hmm,' she said with a new, dangerous edge to her voice. 'If anyone wants to be pessimistic about Joe they'd just better stay out of my way today, that's all I can say. Come on, Joe — let's go sort out this walking issue once and for all.'

I watched her walk off with a determined step, the little dog choking itself as it surged ahead. A few gossiping volunteers turned to watch as Jamilla and Joe walked their way over noisily to a quiet corner of the yard.

'Ah, Jamilla?' called out one of the watching ladies. I saw with interest it was Rude Lady. She coughed. 'Er, no offence but I'm not sure that the way you're doing that is —'

Jamilla didn't hesitate. She simply held up a hand and said, 'Not now, dear — I know perfectly what I'm doing — and if you knew better, you would have already fixed him.'

Rude Lady blinked in surprise and turned to her companion, deeply offended. 'Well!'

I barely stopped myself from cheering. The new, tough-skinned Jamilla had just kicked her first rude arse.

I dropped by at the end of the week to see how she was going. Joe was now walking perfectly on the leash and Jamilla had decided to adopt him herself.

'I'm so glad I got him. Do you know why? He's so sparky it's contagious,' she said in admiration. 'Now if anyone tries to give me a negative comment, why, I just hand it right back to them so quick their head spins. That soon shuts them up.'

If you know you're too sensitive, then it's definitely time to toughen up. Learn to insist that anyone who's pessimistic, unhelpful or destructive keeps their energy-draining comments away from you. The only person who can keep your sacred inner space safe from other people's negativity is you.

If someone demands you become someone you're not, then let them go

Don't change who you are for someone else otherwise one day you'll wake up wondering where the real you has disappeared to. There's nothing worse than looking in a mirror and wondering, why's that stranger living inside my skin?

This is what happened to Gus when he started dating a much younger, very glamorous woman. The day he woke up and looked properly at himself in the mirror was the day his girlfriend tried to talk him into euthanising his old, loyal dog.

Gus was a fit, energetic 49-year-old who enjoyed the great outdoors. He loved fishing holidays and camping out in old shacks. His best mate was an elderly German Shepherd called Santa, who loved going along on every camping trip and had his own, tattered sleeping bag.

Then Gus met Caroline and everything changed.

Caroline was tall and gracefully beautiful. She had an elegant hourglass figure and when she walked into a crowded room every man turned and stared. Gus couldn't believe it when she agreed to a first date. Within three weeks she'd moved into his rather dilapidated old house. No one could see what Caroline and Gus had in common.

But then, bit by bit, Gus found himself changing. Caroline encouraged him to wear expensive suits, get a new haircut, get a new wardrobe of clothes.

One day I saw Gus sitting in the park on an old tree stump, looking a little apprehensive. His old Shepherd, Santa, barked once at me then subsided into happy greeting sounds.

I gave the sweet old fellow a scratch around his old battered ears. 'Hello, Santa, how's tricks?'

The old dog gave me a gentle lick of acknowledgement.

'Everything okay?' I asked Gus.

'Yeah, everything's wonderful, Marty,' he said. 'Just got a few things on my mind at the moment.'

I sat down on a tree stump next to his.

'Got a decision to make,' Gus said at last. 'A new idea of Caroline's.'

My heart sank. 'Oh yes?' Since Caroline had moved lock, stock and barrel into his house, Gus only ever seemed to have an anxious look in his eyes. I also didn't like the way Caroline pretended Santa didn't exist.

'She's pretty insistent that we sell the house and move into a much richer area closer to the city. As for my little brick-laying business — she keeps making noises about me becoming much more ambitious.'

'Are you going camping this weekend?' I asked, trying to change the subject.

'No. Caroline hates camping. She wants to go to some fancy resort this weekend.' He rolled his eyes. 'Santa has to go in a boarding kennel — he'll hate it.'

'He'll survive,' I said reassuringly. 'What about your weekend fishing shack? You can bring Santa along with you the next time you go.'

'Caroline's thinking we should sell the shack,' he said. 'Thinks it's a dump.'

'Do you think Caroline wants you to change a bit *too* much?' I asked.

'To be honest — I feel like I'm on a rollercoaster. I don't know what the hell she's going to ask me to do next.' Then he laughed. 'But — wow! Look at her! She's just so damned beautiful and glamorous. I can't believe she's with an ugly old mug like me. I mean, let's face it — I'm completely out of her league!'

I looked at him. His face showed he was completely under the spell of this new woman in his life and he wasn't going to listen to any advice unless it came out of Caroline's mouth. I slapped him on the back, wished him luck and said goodbye. Gus obviously needed time to ponder his future.

A month later I bumped into him again in the park.

This time his skin was grey and he was obviously distressed as he stared blankly ahead, kneading Santa's patchy old fur.

'What the hell's the matter?' I asked.

'Marty — I looked in the mirror today and I was horrified by the man I saw looking back out at me.'

I sat down beside him. 'What happened? Does it involve Caroline?'

He nodded and took a deep breath. 'She had a massive argument with me this morning and said I was a weak loser who'd never amount to anything unless I cleaned up my act. She said she'd bought a new white lounge suite for the house so Santa had to go.'

'Outside?' I asked sympathetically. 'You can get a dog kennel.' But my heart sank at the thought of old Santa coping with the cold winters.

'No!' he said furiously. 'She wanted him to be euthanased! She said he was a waste of space and he'd outlived his welcome. She said he was ugly, old and farted, and it was depressing watching him totter around like death warmed up.' He hung his head again.

'Oh.' What could I say? Anyone who knew Gus knew how much Santa meant to him. Suggesting that he put Santa down was like suggesting he amputate his own foot.

'So what did you say to Caroline?' I asked, curious.

'Pack your bags and be gone by the time I get back.'

Remember, if you keep allowing someone to change the real you into somebody you're not, then a day will arrive when you have to look in the mirror and meet the eyes of the person you've become. Just make damned sure you can live with that person.

Let go of unnecessary drama and those who create it

A really easy way to uncomplicate your life is to get rid of all the unnecessary drama in it. Ruthlessly kick out anyone who thrives on creating drama. Instead, pick friends you are proud to know. Mix with people you admire. Fill your life with people you love and who also respect you. Choose to spend time with people who make your day a little more radiant just by being in it.

I learned this valuable lesson when I was involved in saving a gorgeous little dog called Bunny from one of the most exhausting dramaholics I've ever met.

Darrell rang me because he had a West Highland Terrier who needed a new home. It took me about three minutes to realise Darrell was a complete dramaholic — he thrived on having drama in his life.

From what he was telling me, he lived in a state of perpetual chaos. The West Highland Terrier was a nine-month old female. There was nothing wrong with her behaviour or health, he assured me, he just had too much drama going on in his life to have a dog.

Suddenly, in the background I heard a woman start ranting in a screeching voice. Anxious yapping started.

'Do you need to go to sort out what's happening?'

'No, no, no,' he said airily. 'That's just Belinda, my girlfriend. She's just a bit furious with me.'

The screaming and high-pitched yapping continued. I raised my voice louder and asked him a few more questions. Next moment a crash came from the phone.

'Darrell?'

Now loud banging noises, punctuated by even louder screaming, started coming from the phone receiver. The yapping reached hysterical new levels.

'Darrell? Are you okay?'

No reply. I slapped the wall in frustration.

'*DARRELL!*' I bellowed into the phone, wondering if he could even hear me.

'Yes, yes, yes,' said Darrell in a soothing voice. 'I'm still here, mate — don't worry. That's my other girlfriend, Louise — she's just broken in through the window. Nothing to worry about. Just a little misunderstanding — seems I asked both of them to move in with me this weekend. Neither of them are very happy about it.'

He took a breath. 'Now where were we? Oh yes — Bunny. She's a real pretty sweetheart.'

Somehow I ungritted my teeth and agreed to meet with Darrell and Bunny in a public car park the next day.

'Don't be late,' I warned him.

Darrell was an hour and a quarter late and by that time I was furious. I was just about to drive off when his car raced into the empty car park and screeched to a halt beside me.

'Why the hell didn't you ring me?' I demanded, annoyed, when he wound down his window.

He smiled soothingly. 'Couldn't ring you, mate — Louise ended up throwing my cell phone out the window last night. Anyway —' he reached beside him and held up one of the prettiest little white dogs I've ever seen, '— meet Bunny.'

My heart melted at the sight of her. She had merry eyes and a tiny button nose and a curling pink tongue. Her white hair was gleaming clean and looked as soft as silk. Her little ears were cocked up and alert.

'She's an utter sweetheart,' said Darrell cheerfully. 'Only reason she has to go is because of a small bit of chaos in my life.'

I didn't bother commenting. Something told me Darrell's life was never less than neck high in chaos.

'Oh well, Bunny, enjoy your new life,' he said cheerfully. I couldn't believe how calm he was about giving up such a gorgeous little dog. He revved his car and was gone in a screech of the tyres.

With Darrell gone, I felt Bunny's little body sag in relief. I placed her down on the ground and she shook off the stress of Darrell from tip to toe.

Bunny's new owner, Betty, adored her immediately. They were perfect for each other.

'A cup of tea for you, love?' Betty asked.

Tea was exactly what I needed to wash away the taste of Darrell and all his needless, exhausting drama.

'Tea would be perfect,' I said gratefully. 'Wow, never invite dramaholics into your life, Betty.'

Betty chuckled as she switched on the kettle. 'Now don't you worry, dear — some people like drama in their life. I reckon it's like a kind of fizzy juice they run on.'

My advice on the subject is this: don't walk away from dramaholics, damn well flee for your life! Let's face it — our time on earth is just too short to spend with people who drain all the happiness and energy out of you.

Are you missing out on human love?

Now don't get me wrong — I think it's fantastic spending lots of time with dogs. However, sometimes I get sad when I see some people lavishing all their love on their dogs. Why?

I feel they're maybe missing out on experiencing the special qualities of human love.

If you're a person who feels safer entrusting all your love to dogs rather than humans, then Dee's story is for you.

Dee asked me to help with her pair of Chinese Crested dogs. You may have seen this graceful toy breed around, they're the little characters without hair on their body and a punk-like crest of hair on their head and ears, with tufted feet and a plumed tail. You really can't miss them! Chinese Crested dogs are affectionate and clever, and Dee's dogs, Chanel and Gucci, were a really lovely female and male pair. Dee was concerned by the occasional tussles they were having. These tussles weren't really fights, they were just little domination scuffles with some baring of teeth.

We discussed a behaviour program that would sort out the tussles and she agreed to try out my suggestions.

'I want my two babies here to be as happy as larks,' she said to me with a charming smile, waving her hand at the dogs. Dee was seventy-three with perfectly coiffed hair, and wore an exquisite dress and very impressive diamonds. She possessed a rich and throaty laugh that was still sexy.

We watched as her two dogs leaped, graceful as ballet dancers, up on the silk damask loveseat that was specially theirs.

'However, I do have one concern, Martin. Are you sure if I try all these suggestions that Chanel and Gucci aren't going to be miffed with me?'

'Not at all. They'll be happy that it's going to be much more peaceful around here. It's so bewildering for dogs if we treat them as equals. You need to start thinking of yourself as their leader.'

She looked at me hard. Carefully and deliberately, she put her coffee cup down on a side table, then sent me a truly charming smile. 'Oh dear — we're going to have a problem then. Because I have *no* intention whatsoever of being Chanel and Gucci's leader.' She said the word with distaste. 'I only wish to think of them as my babies.' Scratch the surface of a wealthy lady and you get a spoilt empress, I couldn't help thinking with a sinking heart. The consultation was rapidly veering toward failure.

'I'm sorry,' I said. 'I thought you understood when I explained earlier. Dogs think differently to humans. Your dogs will only feel truly happy and content when you act as their leader — the Boss.'

She held up an elegant finger, hushing me. 'No,' she said pleasantly. 'No — I will not be their leader and my two dogs will only ever be treated as my babies.'

Okey dokey, I thought in bafflement. This woman's implacable attitude was almost beginning to scare me.

'May I ask if you have children?'

'Yes,' she said. 'Three.' She coughed and flicked a piece of lint off her lap. 'We don't speak these days. Haven't for thirteen years.'

Bloody hell, I thought. Talk about having ice water in your veins. By her calm tone of voice, she could have been discussing a distant relative who hadn't visited for a while. Things were beginning to become clearer — especially when she immediately called the dogs to her.

She held out her hands like an open embrace. 'Come here to Mummy, my darling babies. Chanel? Gucci?'

Both dogs leaped from their chair and ran to her, jumping up beside her then standing on her lap, licking and nudging her for non-stop pats.

'They seem to love me exactly as I am without any of the changes you wish me to make,' she said, challenging me with her cool gaze.

I couldn't be bothered explaining her beloved little dogs were simply dominating her, invading her personal space with their paws and tongues. Or that they were deeply confused by her behaviour.

I stood up to go. 'I think I should go now,' I said very politely. 'Before I waste any more of your time.'

She inclined her head in agreement and went back to allowing herself to be dominated completely by her two dogs. They were now licking her frantically as they picked up the dark, sad energy swirling around their mistress.

As I walked away, I glanced back to see Dee patting and kissing each dog in turn. I tried to imagine not speaking to my own wonderful children for thirteen years, but couldn't. I left Dee to her dogs, who were simply dominating her — not loving her. But she didn't seem to care — all she cared about was getting her next 'love fix' of licks from her dogs.

If you lavish all your love on your dogs and save none for any humans close to you, then I humbly believe you may be creating a sad and empty space inside your heart and mind. If you have plenty of love to give to dogs, then try risking some of it on humans. You may be surprised where loving a human leads you.

Stop expecting to find perfection in dogs — and people

Do you ever wish everyone in your life was perfect? The problem is, such an idea focuses on the wrong things. Perfection implies you don't want anyone in your life ever making mistakes. But is that really what you want? Isn't it better to have people you can trust? Who care for you? People you can relax and have fun with? Who love being around you as much as you love being around them? Instead of looking for perfection, start looking for people who know all about your own mistakes and weaknesses yet stick by you and don't walk away.

If you try to insist on perfection in everyone around you, the story of Claire and her less-than-perfect dog is for you.

Claire walked her dog in the same city park as I did. While I was a bit on the scruffy side with a head full of dreadlocks, Claire was always a walking advertisement for elegant perfection. Her clothes were always white or cream and spotless. Her hair was always a gleaming blonde curtain of silk.

However, every time I noticed a tiny expression of annoyance hovering around her mouth that rather spoiled her good looks. Her cool, assessing eyes seemed to be constantly roaming over everyone and everything — looking for imperfections, perhaps.

Her boyfriend, Damien, was always perfectly dressed in casual, expensive clothes, as you'd expect. Simon, her Maltese Terrier, was a great character, though he was never allowed to have a hair out of place.

One day I'd just walked past Claire, Damien and Simon in the park, when I heard a loud screech of brakes from somewhere behind me and a sickening bump.

I jogged back to where the noise had come from. A car had stopped in the middle of the road, while Claire and Damien crouched around a scruffy white thing lying on the road. A horrified lady emerged from the car and apologised tearfully. 'He just appeared out of nowhere.'

Damien picked up the little dog in his arms and started walking quickly in my direction.

I looked at the still body that seemed to be half-covered in blood. 'Anything I can do to help?' I asked. 'Is he —?'

Damien looked grim. 'He's alive — just. I'm going to race back to my car and get him to the vet as fast as I can.'

I watched as he and a very frightened Claire hurried away in their desperate race to save Simon.

Simon lived. I saw the three of them some months later when they gave Simon his first public walk in the park since his accident. The little dog was hopping slowly along because he now only had three legs. He had a neatly bandaged stump where his fourth leg had been.

Damien looked down at him proudly. 'It was a close shave, but the marvellous vet managed to save him, though not the crushed leg. Isn't he a plucky boy?'

I glanced across at Claire, who was being unusually quiet. She had a smile pasted on her mouth, but her eyes were cool as they slid over Simon. They cooled even more as they roamed with distaste over his new deformity.

'He's going to hop everywhere from now on.' Damien laughed.

I watched them walk off together, wondering how long Claire was going to endure a dog who was less than perfect.

Sure enough, I bumped into Damien walking Simon alone a month later and knew straightaway something was wrong.

'What's up?' I asked him.

He looked at me and I read genuine hurt and anger in his eyes.

'It's Claire and her damned quest for perfection all the time. It's like any sort of imperfection or deformity terrifies her. We've just had an almighty argument and in the end I just had to get out of the apartment.'

'You look pretty shook up.'

'Do you want to know why? Claire just informed me that she's found a new home for Simon — someone she tracked down on the internet.' He could barely contain his outrage. 'She said she can't handle him being so *broken*. She wants to start all over with a new champion Maltese puppy.'

I looked at him in dismay. 'I don't know what to say.'

Damien snorted in disgust. 'Well, I sure did. I told Claire that she'd better wake up to herself and finally face up to the bloody horrible obsession she has with perfection. I demanded to know what she was going to do if *I* ever happened to get an imperfection she couldn't cope with. What was she going to do to me if I started going bald? Or put on a bit of weight? Or have an accident that left me permanently disabled? Would *I* be thrown onto the scrap heap too?'

'What did she say?'

'Not much,' said Damien. 'Because I didn't wait to hear her answer — I just stormed out with Simon and headed here to the park.' He took a deep breath. 'But I am giving her an ultimatum. Either she goes and seeks help about her intolerance to imperfection — or Simon and I are moving out.'

Out of the corner of my eye I saw someone in cream and white approaching. Claire drew to a stop nearby, looking subdued.

'I think Claire's come looking for you both,' I said. 'I'd better leave you two to talk.'

As I walked past, I saw a new look in Claire's eyes. She looked lonely, scared and vulnerable. I think she was ready to change.

It took a three-legged Maltese Terrier to teach Claire what the truly important things in her world were. She could stay in her perfect world but she'd do so alone. Simon's accident was her wake-up call to grow up and accept that the real world isn't a perfect place — thankfully.

Do you try and make people — and dogs — addicted to you?

Do you frantically try your hardest to make people like you? If so, ask yourself why you go to so much trouble. Why can't you simply relax and let everyone enjoy the real you?

Kerry was inspired by his dog to finally shed all his try-hard behaviour and just be himself.

I met Kerry through a dog-rescue group when I was holding a series of workshops for the volunteers at their shelter. His overwhelming charm hit me straightaway.

'Hello, Martin. *Welcome!* Thank you so much for coming today.'

He went on to bring me endless cups of tea, kept up an easy patter of light-hearted jokes and introduced me to everyone — in fact he lavished me non-stop with friendly, warm hospitality. I quickly found his try-hard behaviour very smothering.

I was in the middle of showing a small group of volunteers how to spot when a dog was deliberately manipulating them, when Kerry walked over and started smothering me with charm again. I cut for a short tea break and took Kerry aside so we were alone.

'Look, Kerry,' I said. 'I'm here today because I genuinely want to help this group of volunteers and rescue dogs. You don't have to keep buttering me up with all this charm stuff. To be honest, your behaviour's really starting to get on my nerves. You can't charm me into liking you.' I let that sink in. 'In fact, what you're doing is a subtle form of manipulation. You're trying to force me into liking you by making yourself as pleasant and indispensible as possible.'

He started to protest. I held up a hand.

'Before you say any more — let me give you a demonstration of what I'm talking about.' I walked over to where a volunteer was holding a small Staffy called Boo on a leash.

'May I borrow Boo for a moment?' I asked. She agreed and I led Boo over to a quiet corner with Kerry.

'What do you want to show me?' asked Kerry with a touch of sulkiness in his voice.

'I want to demonstrate how dogs and people can use friendly, nice behaviour to manipulate others,' I said quietly.

I sat down and asked Kerry to join me. Boo immediately closed in on me and started nudging me for pats, licking and leaning against me.

'Watch how Boo uses all this friendly, delightful behaviour as a way of demanding that I keep patting her,' I said.

By now Boo's charming manner was starting to slip as she got more demanding.

'What she's doing here isn't really friendly and affectionate,' I explained. 'The truth of the matter is, she's trying to dominate me.'

Kerry looked at me uncomfortably, then back at Boo. Her licking became more frenzied. The dog was now trying to manipulate him as well.

'So what you're saying is my charm and friendliness is my way of subtly trying to dominate you?' he asked.

'Yes, but in fairness to you, I don't think you're even aware you're doing it. I'm guessing you've done it all your life.'

He raised his eyes, and I saw a much more vulnerable man revealed. 'I don't know how you guessed it,' he said. 'My father was a police officer and we always got moved to new towns. Because I was the dreaded cop's son, I was always afraid no one would like me — not the ordinary me anyway. So I guess one day I just started over-compensating. If someone else could afford to be just a bit funny, I had to be super-funny. If someone else could just relax and be rude sometimes or boring or unpleasant, well, I certainly didn't feel like I could. That's when I deliberately set out to be as charming as possible, I guess.' He shrugged. 'But as a strategy, it worked, didn't it? I survived.'

'But don't you see? You were acting a part. You faked your way through all your childhood friendships. Even now as an adult — you're still not revealing your true self. That's why I don't want any more of your charm.'

He looked at me warily.

I smiled. 'Please — just be your real self so I stop feeling you're trying to manipulate me like Boo. So are we cool?'

He smiled hesitantly. 'Yeah — I'll drop the charm. But I'm a pretty ordinary bloke without it.'

'Are you kidding? I bet with all that moving around and having a cop for a dad you've got stacks of fascinating stories. I think you're the only person who thinks you're ordinary, Kerry.'

He smiled at that, and I liked seeing a new, confident gleam in his eyes.

If you fear you're too ordinary to reveal your true self and overcompensate by being overly charming, funny, helpful or sympathetic, why don't you throw away that exhausted bogus 'you' forever? It's time to relax and let the world enjoy the real you at last.

Do you accidently give mixed messages to those closest to you?

Have you been accused of giving out mixed messages to the people closest to you? If you have, then this story of Michael and Sarah and their dog is for you.

Michael lived in the same apartment block as I did when I was based in an inner-city suburb. He had an elegant fawn-coloured Whippet called Polly. Michael's girlfriend, Sarah, was a frequent visitor and straightaway I enjoyed the company of this happy, affectionate couple.

They were great fun to share an occasional meal with as they got on so well together. But they had one big issue in their relationship: both accused the other of giving mixed messages.

I was at their apartment having dinner when this issue arose yet again.

'I can't wait!' enthused Sarah. 'Michael and I are booking our romantic holiday to Thailand tomorrow.'

'Brilliant!' I said. 'Thailand must be one of the most beautiful places in the world.'

Michael was being unusually quiet. 'Are you looking forward to the trip?' I asked cheerfully.

He glanced at me, then Sarah, then returned to concentrating on eating his meal. 'Sure,' he grunted. 'It's going to be great.'

Sarah gave him a long look and frowned.

'Yes, Martin,' she continued on a determinedly happy note. 'We plan on it being the most romantic getaway we've ever been on. Don't we, honey?'

Michael gave another grunt and kept his eyes down on his food.

Warning bells started ringing loud and clear inside my head. Oh dear, I thought. Wrong response, Michael. Not a good idea to act like this around a woman determined to have a special time.

'Anyone for another helping?' I asked cheerfully, trying to halt the rising tension.

Sarah leaned forward, eyes narrowed, and glared down the length of the table at her boyfriend. 'Michael, you're sending me mixed messages about how you really feel about this holiday. Do you *or do you not* want to come on this holiday with me?'

I wondered whether I should excuse myself before this slid into a full-scale argument.

Michael glared at his plate for a moment, then raised his eyes to look at Sarah. 'I agreed to go,' he said. 'We're booking the damned trip tomorrow — so stop badgering me.'

I stood up swiftly. 'Wonderful dinner. Thanks but I should be going before it gets too late.'

Sarah stood up too. 'I'll walk you to the door, Martin.'

I walked down the hall to the door. Sarah caught up, opening it for me.

'Sorry for wrecking a nice evening,' she said. 'I just start seeing red whenever Michael sends me such mixed messages.' She gently banged the wall to relieve some of her frustration. 'Three weeks ago he couldn't *wait* to go on this holiday — he was even more excited than me. Now look at his reaction to it. He can barely raise a grunt about it.

'I was so excited when he suggested a romantic holiday. I thought we were becoming so close that, well —' She hesitated, then went on in a rush: 'I thought he was planning on proposing to me in Thailand.'

'I think he's just realised you expected a marriage proposal. He's probably feeling too much pressure.'

'Then why on earth did he make such a big deal about how romantic this holiday was going to be?' she asked. 'Sunset walks on the beach? Memories forever? Talking of a ring?'

'You'd better go back in and ask him that,' I said. 'Both of you are going to have to stop assuming you know how the other person feels.'

There was a loud, noisy yawn from below.

I nodded at the dog standing next to us. 'Take Polly here for instance. See how she just yawned like that in such an exaggerated manner? What do you think she's saying to us right now?'

Sarah laughed. 'That we're boring her?'

'No — she's actually feeling extremely distressed right now. She's worried because you and Michael have this argument brewing between you. You see, noisy, exaggerated yawning is one of the ways dogs try to get others to calm down and relax. It's their way of trying to get other dogs to stop fighting.'

'Really? I never would have thought that — not in a million years.'

'True communication can be such a tricky thing, can't it? See how we misunderstand what our dog is trying to say? Sometimes it's just as difficult understanding people — even the people we feel closest to. Why don't you go and find out what Michael wants from this romantic holiday of his. Don't assume anything.'

'You're right. I'd better go and sort out our mixed messages.'

They returned from Thailand engaged and twenty-two years later, they're still happily married.

If you think you're getting mixed messages from someone you're close to, don't get upset and angry, just calmly ask them what they mean.

Your dog knows exactly what kind of friend you are

Have you wondered what you're like as a friend? I believe your dog knows exactly what sort of friend you are because what are our dogs if they aren't our hairiest friends?

When I lived in a country village, one of my neighbours was Gerald, an elderly man with a Dachshund called Max. My other neighbour on the other side was Andy, a young man with a Bullmastiff called Monster. Every day I saw these two men take their dogs out for their morning and afternoon walks. The way each man was with his dog told me a lot about how they conducted their friendships with humans.

If I sat out on my verandah facing the street, I could hear the very different ways these men treated their dogs. I'd hear a click of Gerard's gate and the calm, steady tread of his shoes as he walked down his footpath.

'Come on, Max, old fellow,' he'd say politely to his dog as he walked through the gate. 'Don't dally around, please.'

He'd walk past my house to do a lap of the village. Seeing me, he'd raise a friendly hand in greeting. 'Good morning, Martin. Beautiful weather we're having.'

I always enjoyed returning his greeting, in fact it was a joy watching this lovely, old-fashioned gentleman take his stroll around the village oval and back with dignified little Max trotting along at his side on his leash. Watching them, you could tell this pair were great companions who'd clearly enjoyed sharing this walk for years. I always smiled as I came across them when walking my own dogs. Gerald would be greeting people politely or murmuring in a relaxed conversational way to Max. 'Look at that, will you, old fellow,' he might say to his dog. 'Julie's roses are looking spectacular this year, aren't they?' Or, 'Fancy that, Max — Mrs Peterson's finally getting that new driveway she always wanted.'

Obviously Max had no idea what Gerald was saying but he could tell by his soothing, friendly tone that he was happy and wanting to bond with him by including him in the conversation.

However, a little later, I'd be able to hear Andy taking Monster for a walk. This was done quite differently.

Andy's voice was always far louder than it had to be. 'Come on you dumb mutt, Monster! Get your lazy butt into gear, I've got to get to work and I haven't got time for all this stupid stopping and sniffing. *Move it right now!*'

They'd pass my house heading in the direction of the public park at the end of the road. As they passed, I'd see Andy wrenching and dragging the leash as he tried to use his cell phone at the same time. He believed the walk was the perfect opportunity to check his emails. Seeing me watching him, he'd give me a quick wave. 'Hiya, Marty.' I'd raise a hand politely in reply — but the way he treated his dog didn't make me warm to him.

Once past my house, Andy would reveal even more of his true bullying nature. Poor Monster was actually a very sweet bumbling teenager whom Andy had never bothered to train properly. Andy would impatiently shout at the poor dog and lose his temper with it.

I always thought it significant that how these two men treated their dogs was how they treated their friends too.

Whereas Gerald was an extremely thoughtful man to his human friends, Andy was a bit of a dictator. If one of Gerald's friends needed a helping hand, Gerald was always first at their door in his polite, unassuming way. However, I saw quite a few times that if any of Andy's friends needed his help, they were usually sent away empty-handed. Whereas Gerald was a staunch, loyal, good friend, Andy was more of the fair-weather variety.

One evening I had to visit both men to let them know I was having some tree-lopping done the next day. How I found them with their dogs clarified in my mind what kind of friend each man made.

At Andy's house, I found Monster on a chain in the backyard, sitting miserably in his dog kennel. He might as well have been sent to outer Siberia. Although Monster had a full bowl of food, a full water bowl, shelter in an expensive dog kennel and the best collar money could buy, he certainly didn't have a good friend in his human. I left Andy as soon as I could and made my way over to Gerald's house.

Gerald welcomed me in and urged me to join him for a cup of tea. I was ushered into his living room, where he and Max had clearly been watching TV together. As Gerald sat back down again, I smiled.

'You look happy,' Gerald said pleasantly.

I felt my smile grow wider. 'I was just thinking what great friends you and Max are,' I said.

Gerald patted Max and nodded. 'Yes, this is without a doubt my best friend in the world.'

Like two comfortable bachelors living out their last years comfortably, theirs was a friendship that was indeed inspiring. Take the time to ponder what kind of friend you are, both to your dog and the people in your life.

Your dog versus your partner

Have you fallen into the habit of lavishing far too much affection and attention on your dog rather than on your human partner? It's an easy habit to fall into, isn't it?

Kay and Mitchell were a retired married couple I met as clients because of their gorgeous Australian Silky Terrier, Georgie. Unfortunately, they both treated Georgie as the love of their lives, which led to heart-rending consequences.

Kay rang me up one day, concerned that Georgie was beginning to attack other dogs when out walking.

'She's so good in every other way,' she said. 'But lately she's starting arguments with other dogs down at the park for no reason. I got a real fright today when she suddenly lunged out at a peaceful German Shepherd and acted like a crazy lunatic, trying to rip its throat out. Luckily I was able to pull Georgie off before she got herself killed.'

She took a deep breath. 'Mitch and I just love Georgie to bits. She's the great love of our lives. In fact, she's like our baby now that our two children have grown up and married. We couldn't bear it if anything happened to our darling little girl.'

I agreed to meet Kay and Mitchell at their local dog park the next day to see if I could help them.

From experience, I already had an inkling of what was triggering Georgie's aggression problem. I call it the 'empty nest syndrome' — when the human kids grow up and move away, many retiree couples get a really cute little dog to lavish lots of love on. This is a great idea, except if both partners start giving the dog *too* much affection and attention.

Why is too much love a problem? Once you start treating any dog as though it's more important than the humans around it, the dog quickly develops an inflated sense of self-importance. This is when lots of behaviour problems start popping up. Georgie, I suspected, was being loved too much.

I arrived at the park the next day and walked over and introduced myself.

'This is Georgie, our baby,' said Kay proudly. She fondled the little dog's ears and dropped a kiss on her nose.

Georgie glanced at me without much interest and looked away again, panting rather stressfully.

I soon saw why she was so stressed. I'd been right about the empty nest syndrome.

Both Kay and Mitchell were seated on either side of this small dog trying to out-do each other in the amount of affection they could lavish on her. 'I'll just wipe her mouth — she has some crumbs stuck in her whiskers,' said Mitchell. He pulled out some tissues and fussed with Georgie's whiskers.

'Oh look out,' snapped Kay, 'You're annoying her — let me do it.' There was a tussle over the tissue.

I decided it was time for me to interrupt the discussion before it turned into a full-scale argument. 'Er — how about we take Georgie for that walk now?' I suggested.

They stood up and had a brief argument about who should hold Georgie's leash. Then another argument about which direction the walk should take.

In between these spats, they never stopped kissing, hugging, patting, touching or just looking at Georgie.

I could see the little terrier was absorbing all this overwhelming attention and affection quietly — but I could also see the stress rising in her. She was starting to lick her lips nervously and pant heavily. She was staring with a glazed expression at nothing much, desperately trying to shut out all of Kay and Mitchell's suffocating emotions.

Another argument was starting between Kay and Mitchell over whether Georgie should have a drink before we went for the walk.

'Whoah,' I said. 'Let's take a breather here.'

Kay and Mitchell looked at me.

'This is crazy,' I said. 'Look at you both. This little dog is stuck between the two of you constantly bickering over her welfare.' Then I pointed to Georgie. 'Just look at how stressed she is. She's not a happy dog at all.'

I sat them down and took the dog's leash from Mitchell. Georgie immediately shook herself, desperate to throw off all that human tension and conflict she'd been absorbing from her owners.

'But we *love* Georgie,' said Kay.

'She's the light of our lives,' agreed Mitchell.

'Sure,' I said. 'But at the moment, this poor dog is so confused and stressed by your behaviour that she's started acting up. She has to live all the time with this non-stop tension between the two of you. When the tension grows too unbearable, she has to off-load it somehow — so she attacks other dogs.'

They stared at me in shock.

'I'm not joking,' I said. 'If you like, I can show you a program to change Georgie's aggressive behaviour towards other dogs — but it's not going to work unless the two of you start showing her a united, *happy* household. To do that — both of you have to start showing each other much more affection.'

They looked at each other unenthusiastically.

Mitchell frowned. 'I don't understand. Kay and I love each other — *of course we do* — we're married.'

I let out a deep breath. 'You may be married — but I'm not seeing much affection happening between the two of you at the moment.'

They both stared at me stonily.

My heart sank. Sometimes I get a bad feeling about clients. I sense that no matter what I say — they just aren't going to listen.

'I love Georgie like she's my baby,' said Kay, a stubborn note creeping into her voice.

'All I'm asking,' I said, 'is that you start giving much *more* attention and affection to *each other* than to your dog,' I said soothingly.

Kay laughed scornfully. 'Don't be silly — if I lavished love on Mitch like I do on Georgie — he'd be unbearable! He'd get a real fat head and be impossible to live with.'

'And you'd walk all over me,' snapped Mitchell, glaring at Kay. 'If I ever started treating you like I treat Georgie.'

They stared at each other unimpressed.

'Exactly,' I said, trying to calm everyone down. 'Can't you see this is what you're both doing to Georgie? You're inflating her ego to dangerous levels. She now feels she can tackle big, scary dogs. But look at her — she's only tiny. If she keeps attacking dogs like this she's going to end up getting herself killed.'

'Okay,' snapped Kay, glaring at her husband. 'I'll try your ideas out, Martin. But only for Georgie's sake.'

'So will I,' said Mitchell stiffly.

I quickly outlined a behaviour program for Georgie. She was to get a lot less attention and affection from both her owners from now on. I also showed them how to walk her safely past other dogs. We practised this until I was confident that they could handle Georgie around other dogs.

We agreed to meet the following week at the park so I could check their progress.

Nearly a week had passed when I received the call from Kay that I'd half been expecting — she wanted to cancel our appointment. 'We've bought a new sort of harness,' said Kay over the phone. 'The latest on the market. It's supposed to give you perfect control of your dog.'

She paused. 'I'm afraid we can't bring ourselves to stop spoiling our daring little Georgie, Martin. There's no way I can treat my lump of a husband like I do my lovely little baby girl — and I'm sure Mitch feels the same way about me.' She sighed. 'I guess Georgie's become our safety valve for a relationship — we really *enjoy* being able to love her to bits.'

My heart sank. Some people can't change their ideas about dogs, but I felt I had to warn her one last time.

'Just remember why I'm worried about you and Mitchell spoiling Georgie so much at the expense of your own relationship,' I said. 'If she continues to attack dogs, then one day she's going to pick on the wrong dog and — SNAP! — it'll all be over.'

Kay laughed. 'Don't worry, Martin,' she said airily. 'The new halter's going to solve all that.'

A month later a friend told me that Georgie had been walking with Kay and Mitchell when she darted out in her new halter, attacked a passing dog and was killed in the following fight.

'She and Mitch are devastated,' my friend told me.

I remembered how much Kay and Mitchell had loved their little dog and knew how desperately they would be grieving.

If they do get a new dog, I only hope they don't make the same mistakes as they did with Georgie. Otherwise they'll end up loving another dog to death.

If you think you and your partner might be spoiling your dog more than each other — then perhaps Georgie's story will persuade you to re-think your relationship. Just like us, dogs like to be surrounded by a loving, close-knit family. Nothing will make your dog feel happier, calmer and safer than seeing gestures of love between you and your partner. After all, nobody understands the power of relationship bonding as well as dogs.

Learn to let your love show exuberantly!

No one can deny that dogs know how to give and receive love much more exuberantly than we humans. They just don't hold back any of their enthusiasm, do they? I believe dogs are the perfect teachers to show us why it's worth letting go of our reservations and lavishing love on those who deserve it.

This is how a husband finally learned from his dog how to show his wife the love and affection she deserved.

I met Brad and Mia when they called me out to see their Golden Retriever, Arthur, who was constantly knocking over visitors with his over-exuberant welcomes. I showed them the polite, respectful way I wanted this dog to greet people from now on: sitting calmly at their feet. I got Brad to show me that he could get this result, which he did.

'Your turn now, Mia,' I said cheerfully. 'Show me what you can do with this dog of yours.'

Astonished, I watched her face crumple into tears.

I turned to Brad in confusion. 'Did I do anything wrong?'

I could see from his face he had no more of an idea than I did. As he stood there, I nodded in her direction. Well, go on, my expression clearly said, don't just stand there — go and comfort your wife.

When it was obvious Brad wasn't going to budge, I lost patience and walked across to put my arm around her shoulders.

'What's wrong, darling?' I asked. 'What's got you so upset like this?' I glanced over at Brad but he was still rooted to the spot, with a miserable, shuttered look on his face.

Mia took a few deep, steadying breaths and pulled away slightly from me. 'Oh dear, I'm so sorry.'

I touched her arm gently. 'Come on — tell us what's the matter.'

'I have a confession to make, Martin,' she said. 'I'm probably the reason Arthur's been jumping up on people.'

'Why's that, Mia?'

'To be honest, I've been feeling rather lonely and desperate for affection lately.' She looked at Brad and something passed silently between them.

'So desperate,' she continued, 'that I started encouraging Arthur to give me really outrageously enthusiastic welcomes all the time. When he jumped up on me and wrapped his paws around my shoulders, it was like he was giving me big hugs. Yet you explained earlier that when Arthur hugs me like that he's not really showing me loving affection he's simply wrestling with me in excitement, desperately trying to dominate me.

'I was wondering why his hugs were beginning to get a bit too violent for my taste. He bumped my nose really hard several times and even nipped me on the neck.' She took a deep breath. 'I'm sorry to involve you like this, Martin, but I'm honestly at the end of my patience — Brad, you simply have to start showing me more affection or I'll go crazy.

'Darling,' she said, 'I know you had a tough and unloving childhood, and I know you feel strange showing affection, but I can't go on living in this vacuum. I need you to show me how much you love me.'

Brad stared back at her, then his shoulders sagged. He looked at me in desperation.

I said, 'You heard Mia, Brad. You've got to lose the fear and just let go — show her how you feel.'

They stood so close, staring at each other and I was surprised by the intensity of feelings this issue could still stir deep inside me. This was one of the tough lessons I'd had to learn myself — as I guess most people from violent families have to.

'I'm just not a hugging sort of person,' he said glumly.

'Well, I guess we'll just have to make you into one,' I said briskly. I laughed as an idea came to me. 'I guess if we can make Arthur stop jumping up on people, we can just as easily teach Brad here to become a joyful, welcoming sort of hugger. I guess it'll just take a bit of practice.' I rubbed my chin thoughtfully. 'How about you just keep walking up to him, Mia and open your arms. Brad, you just hug.'

Brad shuffled a little and looked deeply uncomfortable. 'Geez — bit embarrassing, isn't it?'

I slapped him on the back. 'We'll just keep play-acting until hugging feels natural for you.'

After about the fifteenth hug, Brad eventually relaxed and hugged his wife tight — probably for the first time in his life.

It was — as you can imagine — a deeply moving moment.

If you're someone who has real trouble giving and receiving love, it's time to change. Instead of fearing how someone's going to react to your affection, just let go and see what happens. Don't hold back. Openly express your love. If you're happy to see someone, it's time to show it. Look at dogs — they do it so naturally!

Look for someone who loves the real you

One of the most beautiful things about your dog is the way it loves you no matter what. Think about it. Your dog doesn't care what you look like: if you have pimples, or a funny-looking nose, or if you're overweight. It doesn't care if you're not popular or really intelligent. I just love how non-judgemental dogs are around us humans!

One day I parked my car at the big local dog park and let my Irish Wolfhound-cross, Sean, out. I hadn't been here for a while, preferring to walk my dogs along the country lane where my farm is. But today I just wanted to see other people out with their dogs. There were plenty of dogs there that day too.

As I walked across the mowed grass with Sean loping easily at my side, I looked around. There were big dogs streaking around us, small dogs bounding like hares after balls. There were elegant hounds trotting past and strange mixes of mongrels that looked like hairy jigsaws put together wrong. But for me, the one thing that stood out above everything was the utterly beautiful way all these different dogs were looking up at their owners as though these humans were gods and goddesses.

Even when these dogs weren't exactly doing everything their owners wanted, they never for a moment stopped being aware of them. They always knew exactly where their humans were and what they were doing and what mood they were in. It was obvious that every single one of these dogs in the park thought their human was simply the best.

I whistled up Sean and watched as he loped towards me like I was the finest thing in the universe. Seeing his enthusiasm to get back to me reminded me that whenever I'm around dogs I never feel worthless. Our walk over, we headed back to the car. At this moment, the world felt absolutely perfect.

There's nothing like seeing yourself reflected in your dog's eyes. The incredible thing is your dog knows the real you — the moody, difficult bits as well as all the good stuff. And even knowing the difficult stuff, your dog still thinks you're the most wonderful human in the universe.

Improve your relationships by learning to become more observant

How many times have you been accused of not noticing something important by someone close to you? If you want to improve your relationships, start tuning into what's going on around you, especially all the small, easy to miss things that can tell you what's happening in the lives of your loved ones.

I had an unusual day seeing two very different households about their dogs. In one, the humans were completely oblivious to everything around them, while in the other household the humans never stopped watching each other with an eagle eye.

Ted and Raylene called saying their Bloodhound, Lou, had a barking problem and the neighbours were complaining. When I arrived and knocked politely on the door, a deep, blood-curdling baying immediately blasted out at me. Lou. His baying got louder until it was almost deafening. I stifled an urge to cover my ears with my hands. It now sounded like it was travelling up through the ground to invade my head via my feet.

I knocked again. The baying only got louder until it felt like the noise was jack-hammering straight through my brain. No wonder the neighbours were complaining.

The door finally opened to reveal a lady of about sixty. Lou pushed past and sniffed me all over with that huge magnificent nose of his. At least he'd shut up. My ears were still ringing.

The lady looked me over vaguely. 'Yes?'

I introduced myself.

'Oh, yes,' she said. 'Come into the kitchen. Ted and I sit in there.' She ambled down the hall and Lou and I followed.

In the kitchen the large screen TV was on at blaring level. Ted was clearly just as uninterested in my arrival as Raylene. 'Yes?' he said in a gloomy voice in my direction. His eyes kept flicking back repeatedly to his TV.

Again I introduced myself. He frowned, then nodded. 'Yes. You're here to fix Lou.'

I started explaining a behaviour program for Lou that would keep his baying to a minimum. But Raylene and Ted just kept watching TV. I started to feel irritated by their rudeness. They couldn't possibly be taking in anything I was saying. In fact the only one in the room paying me any sort of attention was Lou. He'd laid down at my feet and was sniffing around my legs and shoes as though he'd found the Holy Grail of the Bloodhound world.

'Ted? Raylene?' I asked in an attempt to drag their attention back from the TV.

They didn't hear me, they were so engrossed in the TV. I repeated their names.

They glanced vaguely at me. 'Yes?'

I took a calming breath, but could still feel my teeth starting to clench. 'Are you listening to my suggestions about Lou?'

Ted looked vaguely in my direction. 'Oh, yes, yes — you sort it out. That's what you're here to do.'

I stood up, opened my wallet and placed a business card from the local dog-rescue shelter in the middle of the table where they couldn't miss it. I was clearly wasting my time here. Ted and Raylene didn't even notice as I left. Only Lou padded with me down the hall. I crouched down and fondled his big silky ears that were almost like big curtains on either side of his droopy, lugubrious face.

'I'm sorry, fellow,' I said. 'But your humans aren't going to take any notice of anything I say.' My heart turned over for this magnificent, affectionate dog.

As I let myself out, I decided the humans in this household were the most unobservant I'd ever come across.

My second household visit that afternoon was a completely different kettle of fish.

Gwen and Brendan were divorcing, but had to live in the house together until it was sold. They were worried about their Saluki's behaviour. Apparently, Anna was acting very strangely — lying in corners, facing the wall with her chin on the ground and trembling all over.

The moment I stepped inside the living room, it felt like I'd walked straight into the Antarctic because the atmosphere was so icy between Gwen and Brendan. We introduced ourselves, without Gwen or Brendan looking at each other once. Okay, I thought. This consultation was going to give a whole new meaning to awkward.

Everyone soon arranged themselves into strategic positions around the war zone. Gwen sat on one side of the living room, while Brendan stationed himself in a chair at the opposite end of the room. I sat on the chair in no-man's-land between them.

I glanced over at poor Anna. Sure enough, she'd gone and jammed herself in a corner, nose to the wall, chin on the floor and was starting to tremble all over. My heart went out to her. Like all hounds, she was extremely sensitive and this sort of tension between her beloved humans would be sending her delicate nerves haywire.

I started outlining a program for their dog that took into account their difficult situation and upcoming move to separate homes. They'd already decided to have joint custody of Anna.

The consultation was one of the strangest I'd ever had. Unlike Ted and Raylene, who wouldn't have noticed if their house was on fire unless the TV erupted into flames, in this household, Gwen and Brendan never stopped noticing every single, tiny, subtle thing the other person was doing. They kept a ferocious eagle eye on every facial expression, every movement, every gesture. Why? Each was trying to work out what their enemy was thinking.

Helplessly, I tried my best to keep the peace but their hostility for each other was now too deep. They watched each other as only enemies can, and that well-known saying came to mind: Keep your friends close, but your enemies closer.

In this household, poor Anna had become yet another weapon for them to use against each other.

A few hours later, I reeled out of their home feeling like I'd wandered straight off a battlefield.

It had been an exhausting, unsatisfying day. I'd been to one household where the humans noticed absolutely nothing that wasn't on TV and another household in which the humans noticed entirely too much about each other. Why did it seem on some days that it was virtually impossible for humans to simply communicate with each other — let alone their dog?

If you want to become a good communicator with the people closest to you, then you need to become more observant. Not uncomfortably, ferociously eagle-eyed observant, just enough to show you genuinely care.

Make plenty of time for those who matter most

We're probably all guilty of not appreciating our loved ones enough. Part of the way you can show your appreciation to the people who matter most is by making sure you spend plenty of quality time with them. You'll never know how much your family, lover or friends mean to you until the day they're no longer beside you.

Tim, an extremely successful career man, nearly lost his family — until his dog taught him what mattered most in life.

I met Tim through his wife, Judy. She called me out to ask my advice about the family's dog, a big male Borzoi called Hugh. The vet wasn't having any luck treating an open sore on Hugh's leg, and had recommended that Judy contact me to see if the sores were the result of a behaviour-based problem.

He was right. I showed Judy what I meant.

'Watch Hugh when he lies down — he waits a moment, then starts sucking and licking on that same spot at the top of his leg.'

Judy nodded. 'I see what you mean. How odd.'

'When dogs keep licking in the same spot like this, it's usually because of too much stress in their life. As Hugh feels the tension building up inside him, he tries to find some relief, that's why he keeps mindlessly licking and sucking in one place. Hugh's like a person who keeps scratching at one part of their wrist or arm when they get anxious only he licks and sucks.'

'Okay,' said Judy. 'What do we do now?'

'We find out what's making poor Hugh so stressed.'

She bent her head and stared at her hands.

'Judy?' I prompted. 'Come on — spill the problem, let's sort this issue out as quickly and smoothly as we can.'

'It's my marriage,' she said. 'My husband's job is tearing our marriage apart.'

Tim was a busy advertising executive and his demanding job meant he worked long into the night networking and socialising with clients. On the weekend he was expected to do more schmoozing.

'These days the kids and I barely see him,' said Judy. 'To be honest, we've been arguing quite a lot lately — and that's probably why Hugh's been so stressed.'

'Can Tim put aside a Saturday morning so we can sort out this stressful situation?'

'He'd better. No wonder poor Hugh's feeling so stressed. This job of Tim's is driving me crazy — we never see him any more.'

She rang me later that evening in a more cheerful mood. 'No problem, Martin. Tim agreed enthusiastically to our idea — we'll see you ten o'clock Saturday morning.'

She rang me again early Saturday. 'I'm so sorry, Martin, but Tim's gone and cancelled on us.' She gave a bitter laugh. 'I'm not happy.'

Tim managed to cancel three more appointments, and Judy was getting more furious with each call. 'I'll leave him if he cancels one more time,' she said — and she clearly meant it.

I asked for Tim's number and Judy gave it to me with a scornful laugh. 'See how you go reaching him — these days I talk to his PA more than I speak to him.'

I reached Tim and came to the point quickly. 'Look, I don't want to stick my nose in where it's not wanted. But your wife's at her wit's end trying to deal with Hugh. You really need to keep your appointment with this meeting — or you're not going to *have* a wife any more.'

He was apologetic. He explained things were unusually stressful at work and he was fighting for his job.

'Well, be careful,' I said. 'Because you're about to lose everything that matters most to you — your wife and family — and for what? A job that's thinking of letting you go anyway? Your wife now spends more time with the family *dog* than she does with you.'

'Okay,' he said. 'I hear what you're saying. I'll be at next Saturday's meeting no matter what.'

Much to my surprise, Tim turned up to our consultation and he agreed to find a new job at his family's urging — one that didn't demand every minute of his time.

Once that decision was made you could almost feel the sense of relief that swept through this family group. Even Hugh stopped his frantic leg licking and started to snooze.

Tim thanked me and shook my hand as I was leaving. 'I have a feeling I just narrowly missed having the people who matter most to me walk away,' he said. 'So thanks. Sometimes you just get so caught up in your job, you lose sight of what matters most — the people you love.'

I believe dogs can teach us so much about spending quality time with the people closest to us. Watch how much energy, time and care your dog invests in creating strong emotional bonds with you and the other members of your household. If you're not making time for your loved ones be careful or one day they might just walk out of your life.

Choose a life partner because of compatibility, not just passion

We've all been swept away by crazy, wild passion at some point in our life — and we all love the feeling. But when the time comes for the candles to burn down to stubs and the empty champagne bottle gets tossed in to the recycle bin, it soon becomes clear that you both have to have things in common besides red-hot passion. This is when the natural compatibility between the two of you becomes important. Compatibility is the glue that holds relationships together day to day.

If she'd listened to her dog, Janelle might have questioned whether she was truly compatible with her fiancé, Bryce.

I was called out to help Janelle with her stunning Alaskan Malamute. Apparently her massive male dog, Rum, was causing some friction since Bryce had moved into her house.

I arrived at their house and was greeted by Rum and Janelle.

'So?' I said. 'What seems to be causing this friction between Rum and your fiancé?'

She sighed. 'It was fine when Bryce had his own apartment but now he's moved in with me everything seems to have changed in our relationship. Rum just seems to be the trigger that keeps causing us to fight about how we like things done.' She fondled Rum's ears affectionately. 'I'm even beginning to wonder if we should even get married — Bryce and I don't seem to be as compatible as I thought we were.

'And if it comes to whether Rum or Bryce should stay — well, I'm sorry, but it's no contest. Rum's been with me for six years now — and he's staying.'

I nodded. 'Okay, let's sit down with Bryce and discuss each problem he's having with Rum. Where is he?'

She rolled her eyes. 'Asleep in bed.'

It was eleven-thirty on a Saturday morning. 'Is he sick?'

Janelle laughed. 'Not at all — he always enjoys sleeping in late on weekends. Let me see if I can wake him from the dead.'

Bryce shuffled out and sat with us, and it wasn't long before I realised that Bryce and Janelle were the least compatible couple imaginable.

Janelle loved jogging along the beach early every morning. Bryce could barely be bothered walking as far as the street corner for more cigarettes. Janelle liked meeting new people in big friendly parties. Bryce liked sitting in front of the TV with either his fiancé or best mate for a quiet night in. Janelle was openly affectionate and enthusiastic around people. Bryce was quieter and a bit moody.

It soon became clear that all of Bryce's problems with Rum were because he and this big, enthusiastic dog had completely opposite personalities.

According to Bryce, Rum got up too early. He had too much energy. He was too friendly with strangers. He gave too much affection to Janelle. He simply took up too much room.

I watched how Rum reacted with Bryce and he was aloof and clearly unimpressed with this new male in Janelle's life.

I covered as many behaviour problems as I could with this couple, but I was left with one lasting impression of these two people: they should never get married — they were just too incompatible.

Let them figure it out for themselves, I thought with relief as I got into my car.

I saw Janelle and Rum emerge from their house and they simply looked happy being together. Janelle clipped Rum's leash on and the pair of them walked briskly up to my car.

'Thanks for all your help, Martin — I feel like I understand Rum so much better. We're just getting out for a walk. It's far too beautiful a day to be stuck inside.' She waved cheerfully, Rum grinned happily at me with his huge tongue lolling out, and they walked away — the dog's massive plume of a tail waving to a jaunty beat.

If Rum was a human being then Bryce wouldn't have stood a chance of marrying Janelle. It was becoming increasingly clear to me that Janelle was far more compatible with her dog than her fiancé. If she'd only listen to Rum,

I thought, she'd realise she and Bryce were destined for a rocky future.

I believe that before you commit yourself to someone you want as your life partner, take the time to test your compatibility by living together first. Think about it. Once you're living together and the passion starts to cool, you'll need to find an alternative glue to hold the two of you together — especially on the bad days. I call that glue compatibility.

6

What can dogs teach us about spirituality?

To me, spirituality is wondering about how each of us connects with the universe around us. I don't believe you can own a dog and *not* discover some sort of spirituality within yourself. While taking my dogs for long rambling walks, I've experienced some of the most spiritual and profound moments of my life. As I've wandered with my dogs along beaches, country lanes and city parks, I've found myself falling into a sort of meditative trance, leaving my mind free to roam across spiritual subjects ranging from questions about life and death, why I'm here on earth and what destiny I've been designed to fulfil, to how much I matter and not matter within the universe, and what makes me spiritually happy and at peace with myself.

These stories explore how your dog can help you feel a much stronger spiritual connection with the universe.

Do you live in Me World?

To feel spiritually aware, you first need to step out of Me World so you can find a way of connecting with the much bigger picture. Unfortunately, some people never seem to be able to drag themselves out of the tiny bubble that revolves around them.

I met Zara on a group camping trip with her dog. She lived completely and utterly in Me World, and I have to say, her world seemed like a very lonely place indeed.

The group was spending three days trekking in the Australian wilderness with just our backpacks, tents and dogs on leashes. As I was desperate to see more of the Australian bush, I signed up with my favourite Irish Wolfhound, Sean.

At the place where we parked our cars, we got to meet our fellow travellers for the first time. I looked around: it was like throwing together a camping store with a dog show. There were about thirty people who'd signed up and maybe forty dogs altogether. There were plenty of mongrels, as well as quite a few fancy purebreds.

'Hi, I'm Zara,' said a young woman with a bouncing mop of blonde corkscrew curls. She thrust out her hand at me. 'And this is my Maremma, called Bastian. I can't *wait* to get out into all that wilderness. I'm planning on really tuning into the universe on this trip — it's going to be so spiritual, I just know it is.'

I smiled politely and slipped away. Something about Zara hit me as being far too manic and self-centered to be very spiritual — and I had no desire to spend this trip listening to a total chatterbox. However, as I walked off I noticed that Zara's dog, Bastian, looked like an extremely wise, kind dog. He kept glancing at his mistress like she was a wayward child and he was a responsible nanny.

The next two days were brilliant. The big river country was stunning: the bush tracks wound their way beneath huge gums and at night the stars were incredibly bright. Giant colonies of bats swept past overhead. We saw huge fish and rare platypuses and amazing birds. The dogs were thoroughly enjoying themselves too, despite being kept on leashes.

All of us felt the tranquility of the vast bush seeping into us like magic — except for Zara. Her voice was like a drill that no one could switch off. As I walked through the bush, I kept hearing snatches of her conversation drifting back to me.

'My neighbour's having this argument with me at the moment — his stupid trees are blocking out my morning sun ... '

'... but I can't get a boyfriend at the moment because of my stupid job working in a late-night café ... '

'That Zara, she makes my ears want to bleed,' grumbled an elderly lady with her fat, wheezing Pekingese waddling valiantly beside her.

I had to agree with her. The trouble with Zara was she lived in a self-centered bubble — Me World.

While everyone else in the group found themselves being drawn in by the awesome wilderness around us, Zara just dragged Me World around with her. By the end of the second day, there wasn't a person in the group who didn't want to strangle her.

On the third day, Zara was saved by her dog.

I was directly behind Zara at the time. We were walking in single file when I noticed a huge black snake slithering right across the track in front of her. Zara, meanwhile, was oblivious. She was deep inside Me World and was just in the middle of moaning about her landlord when Bastian, seeing the snake, barged past and knocked her off her feet so she fell backwards out of harm's way. My dog Sean instantly darted forward, ripping the leash out of my hand. He shook the snake and snapped its neck, killing it. Sean came back to me wagging his tail and I patted him in thanks.

Zara got to her feet and gave Bastian a hefty kick in the guts. 'You stupid dog! Why did you knock *me* down you idiot?'

I gave her a look of disgust. 'That's why,' I said, pointing to the huge dead snake.

She gasped at the enormous length of it. 'Hell! I didn't even notice it. Bastian — why didn't you tell me there was a snake there, you dopey dog? I couldn't see it.'

Thoroughly sick of her, I pushed past. 'No — I'm sure you didn't,' I muttered under my breath. 'You're never going to notice anything at all going on outside Me World.'

That afternoon, as we arrived back at our parked cars, I walked past Zara. She was talking to another camper.

'That was such a spiritual adventure for me,' she was boasting at the top of her voice. 'I feel so tuned into the universe right now.'

I watched Bastian sniffing around in the leaves, taking in such an incredible amount of information from just this one small patch of earth. Meanwhile beside him, his mistress continued blabbing on, oblivious to the fact that no one was listening to her.

If I had to choose out of Zara and Bastian who was genuinely tuned into the universe — well, I knew who I'd choose.

If you suspect you live in Me World, then it's time to break out of your self-centered bubble so you can discover all the incredible ways you fit into the vast universe beyond yourself. Your dog will help you do this if you follow its example.

As I grow older, I've come to believe dogs are very spiritual creatures. Watch your own dog playing and exploring in the great outdoors and see what you think.

Enjoy living in the moment

It's so easy to get caught up in creating a successful future that you can forget to enjoy the now.

An ambitious married couple with just that problem decided to get out of their rat-race pursuit of a successful future and start living in the moment — all for the sake of their little dog.

Miriam and Angus called me out to see their Bichon Frise, Benji, when he started night barking for no reason. A Bichon Frise is one of those lively white dogs who looks like a collection of cotton wool balls stuck together. When I heard about the barking problem, I was surprised because this breed is not normally yappy.

We made an appointment for an evening after they'd finished work.

'That'll be at nine pm,' said Miriam. 'Is that too late for you, Martin?'

'You work late,' I commented.

She laughed in amusement. 'Oh — getting home at nine is actually an *early* night for us. We often don't get home till midnight. If you want to get on and win success, you've got to work hard.'

I was beginning to get an inkling of what might be causing the dog's problem.

'If you get home so late,' I asked, 'how do you walk your dog of an afternoon?'

'Oh — we have Lisa,' said Miriam. 'Professional dog walker. She's very good.'

The warning bells were going off inside my head now. 'And how often does Lisa walk Benji?' I asked with a sinking heart, already fearing the answer.

'Every day, twice a day,' said Miriam. 'Seven days a week.'

'And you and your husband?' I asked.

'Oh, we don't have time to *walk* our dog, Martin — don't be silly. We're too busy working to waste our time on that sort of thing . That's what Lisa's for.'

'Of course,' I said. Really — sometimes I wonder why some people even bother owning dogs, they see them so little.

I arrived at their apartment for our appointment and Miriam let me in. She and her husband, Angus, looked exactly like what they were: very successful, ambitious career people on a fast track to huge wealth. Little Benji was gorgeous — and clearly an affectionate, lively fellow. I thought he must be incredibly bored being stuck inside this luxurious apartment most of the day while his humans were at work.

I joined Miriam and Angus in their living room that overlooked the lights of the city. Kicking off bluntly, I told them they weren't spending enough time with Benji. He was lonely, bored and desperately trying to get *some* sort of attention from them by barking at night, as everyone slept — it was the one time they couldn't afford to ignore him. I said their options were limited. They could either find Benji a new home — or they had to give up their crazy, hectic lifestyle.

Miriam and Angus looked at me in horror.

'Give it up?' asked Miriam. 'Not likely — do you have any idea how *hard* we've worked and how hard we *still* have to work to get where we want to be?'

'I can guess,' I said. Benji walked over to me and I fondled him behind the ears. 'But poor Benji here is paying the price for your success.'

There was a moment of heavy silence.

'We'll have to discuss this between ourselves,' said Miriam. 'We'll get back to you with our answer, Martin. How about we let you know in a week?' We all stood up and I was soon catching the elevator down to my car in the parking area.

I thought about the lifestyle Miriam and Angus had created. It sounded exhausting. All their talk had been about when they were going to finally 'arrive' at some point in their successful future. They never mentioned anything about enjoying the now.

Much to my surprise, Miriam rang up a week later and explained that she and Angus had taken stock of their lives, listened to what I had said about Benji and had decided to take off for a weekend getaway to make some big decisions about their future. Benji was coming along too.

'I'm not promising anything,' said Miriam. 'But we've actually become very intrigued about the idea of stepping out of the rat race and seeing what happens to us. Benji being so distraught has really got us reevaluating our own lives.'

The following Tuesday, Miriam rang again. She immediately thanked me.

'This weekend was an incredibly spiritual experience,' she gushed. 'Being with Benji, feeling how great it was to be just enjoying each moment as it happened.' She paused. 'Angus and I have both been so caught up with planning and working towards our future that somewhere along the way we forgot to take time out to enjoy ourselves.

'Angus and I felt like this weekend was our epiphany — you know, that moment when you suddenly and unexpectedly rethink your whole life. As we walked through the ancient rainforest with Benji, we started wondering what we were doing with our lives — and if it was worth the price we were paying.'

I was astounded by the change in this couple. It was like they'd had a complete turn around in their way of thinking. 'So what did you decide?' I asked. 'Is Benji staying?'

She didn't hesitate. 'Believe me, the crazy lifestyle's getting dumped as soon as it can. Darling Benji's staying. In fact, I think he's going to be responsible for saving our sanity and our souls.'

I congratulated her and felt completely dazed as I hung up the phone. It just goes to show that people can always surprise you.

If you fear your life has become a manic rat race in the pursuit of wealth and success, why not take a holiday somewhere surrounded by the great beauty of the outdoors? Perhaps it's time for you to step off your treadmill as you race towards your glamorous future even if it's just for a weekend. Who knows? You might have an epiphany and realise how incredibly fulfilling it is to just live and enjoy each moment as it happens. Living in the now is a powerful way of connecting spiritually to the world.

It's time to find your spiritual strength and toughness

Dogs have taught me to find my own spiritual strength and toughness. You need these qualities to keep you making good decisions in life. In the past when I made easy, weak decisions I always felt bad deep inside myself. However, even at my lowest points when I wasn't proud of my choices, I only had to spend time with a loyal dog and I'd be reminded of all the qualities I admire in dogs — and humans for that matter. Inspired, I'd try to be a better person and make better choices.

I met Trevor in a café and I truly came to admire him during our conversation. When I asked who'd helped him find such incredible spiritual strength and toughness, he pointed to his dog and said, 'Old blind Ding here.'

I looked down and beside him was a small white Cattle Dog-cross, speckled all over with blue spots. I was fascinated. The dog was a bit on the puny side but he held himself with

an amazing, calm dignity. In fact, I'd go further than that —
I'd say he was surrounded by an aura of complete tranquility.
He was an incredibly relaxing dog to be around.

I remarked on this to Trevor and he laughed. 'He sure is
a tranquil dog — you're right there, Marty.'

Trevor told me he was a former drug addict and alcoholic
street kid who'd sold sex to pay for his drug habit.

I looked at him in surprise. Although he certainly looked
on the skinny side, and had quite a few scars on his face, he
was such a calm man it seemed unbelievable that he'd ever
suffered a tough, hard life.

'What do you do now?' I asked.

'These days I work with a charity,' he said, finishing his
eggs and bacon. 'I walk around the city streets and my job
is to save as many street kids as I possibly can. I get them to
eat properly. Get them into drug rehab when they're ready.
Get them on a plane or a bus or train and get them away
when they're ready to get out of the city and stay with some
sympathetic relative. I'm the one they come to for help if
they won't go near a social worker or copper.'

'Wow,' I said. 'That's amazing. And Ding? Does he walk
around the streets with you?'

He laughed. 'Of course. Old Ding never leaves my side.
He's even protected me a few times when pimps have gotten
annoyed with me.' He shrugged. 'They always get annoyed
when I get their best working girls onto buses with an
interstate ticket.'

'I bet the street kids love Ding,' I said. 'The sort of
tranquil energy emanating from this dog is more relaxing
than any drug.'

'Yeah — I always say patting Ding beats any legal or illegal tranquillisers. He's the reason I was finally able to kick the drugs years ago myself.'

'Your spiritual strength and toughness is incredible. I can't feel anything negative coming off you at all — no aggression, no anger, no frustration, no sadness. How on earth do you do it, especially living and working around here? It must get you down sometimes.'

He hesitated, then said, 'Now, you'll think I'm crazy, Martin, but I learned how to keep my soul tough and strong through Ding. Without that spiritual toughness and strength, I'd never be able to keep on helping my street kids — I'd just burn out.'

He fondled the dog's silky ears in appreciation. 'I got him from a rescue group volunteer. When I went around to her house there was this young blind dog. The lady volunteer had called him Ding because she said that was the sound his collar made every time he accidently hit a wall in her house and bounced off again.'

I couldn't even imagine what life must be like for a blind dog. Trevor threw his bacon fat scraps on the ground near Ding and the dog gobbled them up, then relaxed again.

'See that?' asked Trevor. 'See the way that amazing dog just relaxes like that when he wants to? Well, that's how he gets through in life, it's his way of surviving. When all the other rescue dogs used to get annoyed at him or try and pick on him, he'd just go neutral, so all their aggression simply washed over him. Funnily enough, they soon learned to leave him alone.

'Ding's calmness is his armour — it switches off other dogs' aggression. He simply throws himself on everyone's mercy and look how well he does for himself. Better than all the bluff and aggression in the world.'

Trevor grinned at me. 'That's what I call spiritual strength and toughness — and I'm not ashamed to say I try to model myself on Ding every day. Matter of fact, he's my teacher and guru.'

He stood up. 'Anyway, Marty, I've got to go — there's a girl who's been reported bashed by her pimp and she's supposedly gone into hiding. She might take my advice to get into rehab while she's feeling sad and sorry for herself.'

I couldn't envisage facing such dark, thorny problems every single day, and decided Trevor must have unimaginable spiritual toughness and strength to be able to follow such a calling.

I walked with them back to Trevor's van. Fascinated, I watched as Ding calmly followed at Trevor's heel, obviously using his nose to guide him.

'This is my fancy chariot,' Trevor said as he walked up to a rusty, dented van and gave it a fond slap.

There was a handmade poster sticky-taped on the inside of the back window. Trevor said he'd found the quote on the internet and paid one of his street kids to make up the poster. In cheap paint and glitter pens, it read: 'Toughness is found in the soul and the spirit — not in big muscles and small, immature minds.'

I couldn't agree more.

How to age beautifully

Have you ever met an old dog that just has a beautiful aura around it? Although its muzzle might be turning white and it's stiff on its legs and its tail doesn't wag so energetically, there's this gentle kindness around it? I love elderly dogs like these. They're so relaxed and happy and do everything in their power to help you feel like that too. These are the dogs with lovely old souls and I believe we can learn a lot from them about how to age beautifully.

One such dog I've met in my life was a small black Staffy called Lily. She was owned by my friend, Caroline, a ferociously independent lady who had had polio as a child and was left with a permanently twisted spine.

Caroline refused to let her severely damaged body stop her living life to the full. She married, had four strapping sons, had a meaningful career as a psychologist, lived a boisterous lifestyle on a large property covered in rainforest and even helped build her family home. Lily the Staffy arrived as a pup when Caroline's husband decided he wanted a divorce and the freedom to travel the world on his own.

As Lily grew into adulthood, Caroline's sons started leaving home, one by one for university. Soon, Lily and Caroline were the only one's living on the isolated rainforest property.

I met Lily as an elderly dog of twelve years when I first visited Caroline's home. By this time Lily was looking a bit moth-eaten around the edges, was slightly wobbly on her feet and she was slowly going blind, but she had such a sweet, gentle, generous soul that you couldn't help but be charmed by her.

On my first visit, I saw her calmly doing everything possible within her power to make Caroline's life as easy and trouble-free as possible. She greeted me at the front door and escorted me through the house to find Caroline. She brought Caroline her gardening shoes to put on before we went for a walk. She even made no fuss as she killed a deadly Brown Snake on the back verandah while we were having lunch. Then, after lunch, she showed great patience and gentleness while Caroline's young granddaughter, Emma, dressed her up in baby clothes for an hour or so, using the dog as a kind of living doll.

In all that time, the elderly dog rarely took her eyes off her beloved Caroline, as though constantly checking on her well-being.

'Lily never stops watching you, does she?' I asked Caroline as I was leaving.

She laughed. 'She's like my nanny. She worries about me, you see. With my gammy leg I'm always over-balancing, especially when I get over-tired. Living on my own can be a bit of a problem because there's no-one to pull me to my feet again.' She fondled the old dog's ears and smiled down at her loyal friend. 'Dear old Lily here is almost blind now, but she always follows me around using her sense of hearing and smell. If I have an accidental tumble, she sits patiently next to me while I catch my breath and doesn't laugh while I roll around on the ground trying to get back up on my feet. She can fetch me my walking stick if I need it to lever myself off the ground — and if I can't — well, she can fetch me my cell phone so I can ring for help.'

Caroline gave me a crooked grin. 'Of course, I'll have to leave this darling place when Lily's gone. I simply won't be able to manage living in such an isolated spot without her help. But for now, I'm lucky, Lily allows me to keep my independence out here a little longer. She's been the most wonderful companion for me. I almost feel as though she's become a kind of older, wiser, endlessly helpful sister to me. Does that sound strange?'

I looked down at the little Staffy with the grey muzzle and cloudy eyes and a rather pot-bellied belly.

'I think she has one of the most beautiful personalities I've ever seen,' I said truthfully. 'Do you know what? I don't think I've ever met such an unselfish dog before in my life. She really is something special, isn't she?'

Caroline smiled down at Lily. 'Oh, I'm a better person for knowing her,' she said simply. 'I have absolutely no doubts about that. She's taught me how to be the best person I can be, someone I can be proud of.'

Old dogs with beautiful souls like Lily are a real inspiration to me. They remind me that as I get older, I too have the chance to be the most beautiful person I can inside my heart. These days, I find I'm leaving my ego behind more often, and instead, I'm listening more to my conscience as I try harder to be a better person.

I suggest that you also be inspired by the wonderful old dogs you meet. Explore all the good qualities such dogs possess, such as calmness, dignity, honour, loyalty, kindness, gentleness, courage, wisdom and compassion. Be amazed as these admirable qualities begin to radiate out of you as the strongest and most inspirational sort of beauty. Watch as you also begin to draw out the best in the people around you. As you get older and wiser, let all your most beautiful qualities shine from your eyes and inspire the people around you.

That's what I call ageing beautifully.

For all the beautiful old dogs like Lily I've met over the years — thank you. You've helped me become a man I can be proud of.

What are your thoughts doing to your spirit?

Wherever you are, whatever you're doing, choose thoughts that mend your heart rather than shred it. I used to walk my dogs along a busy beach path that followed the Pacific Ocean and I'd fall into the habit of walking with different people. As my dog walks are my sacred time to renew my spirit, it soon became very obvious which people were healthy to walk with and who'd suck the energy from you and leave your spirit shredded and shrivelled.

Some people really stood out. For example, Julius instantly lifted my heart on sight, while Lynn caused my heart to plummet like a stone and got me hurrying in the opposite direction as fast as my legs could carry me.

Lynn walked her merry little miniature Schnauzer along the coast path every day. Despite her dog, Buzz, being a happy-go-lucky fellow who was pleasant to everyone he met, Lynn had a disheartening habit of rehashing all the worst news headlines: gloomy subjects like train crashes, cancer patients suffering agonising deaths, children being murdered by their parents and huge famines crossing nations were all picked over by her with morbid delight. No matter how I tried to steer the conversation away to more pleasant things, Lynn would quickly return to tragic, horrible subjects — all things that tore at my heart and made walking with her a truly horrible, depressing experience.

I'd see the Pacific Ocean glimmering beautifully beside me but all I'd be hearing from Lynn was a string of grisly events. Our last conversation included subjects like rape, a bus crash, someone famous being diagnosed with an inoperable cancer, and a company that had just sacked a thousand employees. My heart felt so shredded afterwards that I promised myself never to walk with Lynn — or anyone like her — ever again.

It was a pity, because I adored Buzz. As I'd see him approaching, my heart would naturally lift and I'd start smiling. However, the price of Lynn was much too high, so I walked a different route to avoid her and her gruesome conversations.

Luckily I did find a much better walking companion. On my new walk — that went in the opposite direction to Lynn's — I met up with an elderly gentleman who, sure enough, enjoyed conversations that made my heart soar.

This gentleman's name was Julius and he had a very dignified, elderly Pug called Patrick. Julius only talked about lovely subjects, like his wife, Margaret, whom he still loved after fifty-four years of marriage, his grandson learning to ride a bike, a bird he could see feeding in a nearby tree, a nice pasta recipe he'd just discovered. He shared the same belief as I did: that our daily dog walks were a time to replenish our spirits, so there were to be no horrible subjects discussed. This was a sacred, tranquil time where we could unwind surrounded by earth, ocean and sky.

One day I remarked that Patrick was a wonderfully calm dog.

Julius smiled down at his Pug and said, 'Ah — Patrick and I have an understanding. We've both decided that we want to live out the rest of lives peacefully, full of serenity.'

Julius wasn't exaggerating, either. I never saw Patrick fight any dog. He'd just calmly walk away from ugly, aggressive behaviour, totally serene within his mind and skin. Watching this dignified dog's decision to live a serene existence, I felt nothing but admiration. His thoughts radiated out of him and calmed down other usually aggressive dogs.

Meeting Lynn and Julius — and their dogs, Buzz and Patrick — made me realise just how much your own thoughts radiate out from you, affecting not only yourself but others. Lynn could have learned from her merry dog, Buzz, how to go through life with a cheerful attitude — but she never did. In fact, I could never understand how that dog's joyful nature never managed to rub off on her — she remained strangely immune to Buzz's happiness. Julius said he'd been most impressed by Patrick's serene attitude and had decided to adopt it for himself. How both these people thought had completely different results. While Lynn caused people to hurry quickly in the opposite direction, Julius drew people naturally to him like a magnet.

So ask yourself: Do you lift people's hearts when they see you? Or do you scare them away with your negative conversations? Are your thoughts nurturing or toxic? You choose the subjects that flow endlessly through your mind, so whether you keep your mind clean and beautiful or pollute it with ugliness, it's up to you.

Look at your dog. I don't think I've seen a dog thinking toxic thoughts — have you?

Do good deeds bring angels into our life?

Nobody could believe in angels less than me — but there've been times I've witnessed miracles that made me pause to reconsider.

I genuinely believe that a scruffy, elderly Labrador called Poppy, who lived in my old neighbourhood, was the closest thing to an angel you can get. I believe this dog was an angel that came into my life at the exact moment she was needed.

Poppy had reached that age where she'd turned pure white. Her fur was slightly fluffy, her muzzle getting a bit moth-eaten and she was beginning to have trouble with her hips. At the time, I lived on the edge of a country village and Poppy lived a few doors down from me.

A busy highway sliced through the town and rich countryside. Although the road was a safe sixty kilometre zone, tired drivers would whizz past much faster than the speed limit and huge convoys of semi-trailer trucks would roar past at high speed. Lee and I lived in a tiny cottage overlooking the highway and we had two daughters and a son. Terrified that the kids and our three dogs would get out on the dangerous road, Lee had insisted we have a high safety fence installed around the house.

Poppy's owner, however, had no fence around her property, so Poppy got into the habit every morning and every afternoon of wandering around the neighbourhood to scent-mark. Sometimes she'd risk convoys of thundering semi-trailers to calmly waddle along the narrow verge of the highway, making her slow way past our house to wee on every letterbox up our end of the village. I could never believe how much road sense she had. She'd stop and look both ways before crossing the highway and she never wandered off the road verge that she was walking along.

However, Poppy did have her enemies. She'd gotten into the habit of knocking over bins on bin night and going through the garbage in search of food scraps. Some people hated how she wandered freely through their front gardens, scent-marking on their letterbox each time she passed. Other people simply disliked dogs. Many was the time I saw old Poppy getting chased down a driveway by a householder shaking their fist at her as they shouted: 'Get out of here, you damned useless dog!'

I always had a soft spot for Poppy. She was a gentle, kind dog who wouldn't hurt a fly. Whenever I'd walk past her, I'd stop and give her a friendly hello and a scratch behind the ear. She'd look up into my eyes and smile her happy Labrador smile. She couldn't help being born so greedy and she was just obeying her natural instincts to roam around the neighbourhood.

One day a disgruntled neighbour came across to me while I was scratching Poppy behind the ears. 'Dunno why you waste your time being nice to that stupid, fat dog,' he grumbled. 'What it needs is a bloody good kick up the arse.'

I just smiled politely at him and continued scratching a grinning Poppy.

What she really needed was a fence. Her frantically busy owner kept promising everyone she'd get one installed as soon as she found the time and the money.

Thankfully for our family, she never got around to it.

Seven o'clock one morning, I was rushing around getting ready for work when I heard a strange yelping cry coming from the bottom of our driveway.

'That's weird,' I said to myself. I kept getting dressed because I was running late.

Again there came that strange yelping cry, but sharper this time.

I was trying to remember where I'd left my work boots the previous night, but something about that sound made me pause.

It came again. Every instinct I possess that's tuned into dogs told me that a dog was down at the bottom of my driveway and it was desperately trying to catch my attention. I ran outside in my bare feet and bolted down the driveway to see what was happening. As soon as I rounded the curve in our driveway, I stopped dead.

My eyes took in a nightmare scene within a blink of an eye — a terrifying image I never want to see again as long as I live.

My three-year-old daughter, Casey, still in her pyjamas, was struggling to get past Poppy and onto the highway. Non-stop semi-trailers were thundering past. Somehow Poppy was stopping Casey from walking that last deadly metre onto the tarmac. She was frantically licking Casey's face to blind her and was blocking her tiny wriggling body from moving forward, using her bulk as a barrier.

Everything went into slow motion as I rushed down and grabbed Casey up in my arms. Trucks roared past, completely unaware of us.

I moved back up the driveway and sank down to the ground in shock, still cradling Casey in my arms. Poppy waddled over and started licking my face in concern, her fat body shaking off the stress she'd just been through.

'Oh Poppy — you clever, wonderful angel,' I remember saying. 'Thank heavens you happened to be in the exact spot and at the exact moment you were needed.'

Incredibly, Poppy, who'd never lived with children, still knew to stop my daughter Casey from going on the road.

That's why I feel I can never completely discount the idea of angels. If there are such things, then I've met one and her name is Poppy. Elderly, fluffy, fat, greedy and with bad hips, but an angel who made a miracle happen for my daughter Casey.

Is this your last day on Earth?

One of the most difficult decisions any dog owner has to make is deciding when to let a problem dog be euthanased by the vet — especially when it's a healthy dog. I've had to help many distraught owners make this tough decision. Once we decide the dog can't be saved, I help the owner ensure that their dog's last day on Earth is as enjoyable as possible. Such days are filled with a sense of profound awareness of the incredible power of life and death, and I always find myself asking: Could this be *my* last day on Earth?

On one occasion, a rescued Rhodesian Ridgeback was standing in front of me, his tearful rescue volunteer, Nicole, clutching his leash as I reluctantly decided his fate.

'I'm sorry, darling,' I said, 'but Dillon here isn't going to make it. He's just too aggressive. He hates children and other dogs and he's going to be too much of a risk for anyone to own. To be honest, I can't believe you haven't had a tragedy on your hands before now. How long did you say you've been caring for him? Five months?'

'I did have a few close calls,' Nicole admitted. 'He nearly gave me a heart attack when my next-door neighbour's four-year-old daughter somehow climbed into my backyard.'

I shuddered at the thought of what Dillon's sharp teeth could have done to that little girl if Nicole hadn't happened to have spotted her in time.

'Dillon's far too dangerous to keep alive,' I said firmly. I took the leash from her trembling hands and went and tied the dog up on a post under a shady tree. I stood back and looked at the dog. 'It's a pity because he's such a magnificent animal.'

'I just feel so guilty and frustrated that we can't help him,' said Nicole, and burst into tears.

I gave her a big hug. 'Hush. You've done everything you could. Most people wouldn't even have tried this hard to help him. Let's just work out a way to make his last day on Earth as enjoyable as possible before he gets put to sleep. What does Dillon like most in the world?'

'He loves going for a run on the beach, he loves chicken mince and he really enjoys chewing a bone,' said Nicole sadly.

'Well, we'll make his last day as enjoyable as possible,' I said. 'We'll give him a lovely slap-up meal of chicken mince for breakfast, then a bone to chew on, then take him for a really good run along the beach on his leash.'

Now the tough stuff. 'We'll arrange with the vet so we can walk straight in without waiting. Then we'll get the sad deed done with the least amount of stress for the dog. You can't bawl or get hysterical beforehand — it's all about making this day as pleasant as possible for Dillon.'

'How on earth am I going to stop myself from bawling?' said Nicole.

'Because your calmness and happiness is going to be your last gift to him.'

She took a calming breath. 'I'll give Dillon that gift,' she said. 'I'll make sure he has the best damned last day of his life.'

And she did.

As I held Dillon's head and the vet gently gave him the green needle, I felt the life force slowly leave him. There came that profound moment when life became extinct in the space of a mere breath. I closed my eyes for a moment. As always, this moment was a powerful reminder of how lucky we are every day.

No matter what else is going on in our lives, it's all so petty compared to the alternative of death. Every day we're given the ultimate gift of all — the gift of life.

I rubbed Dillon's still warm neck in thanks.

Thank you for reminding me how lucky I am.

Live today as though it might be your last day on Earth — with joy and pleasure and gratitude.

Take the time to feel your soul's desires

Many of us don't really know what we want in life, we just feel a vague sense that something's missing. Or perhaps we envy what someone else has. Other times, it feels like we have a hole in our lives that we should be doing something about.

If you ever feel like this, then your soul is begging you to find out what you most want to do in life.

I met Christina at a party and she told me this story.

'It all started,' she said, 'with my Chesapeake Bay Retriever, Duke.'

If you're not familiar with Chesapeakes, they just love — and I mean *love* — to swim. They were bred for retrieving any game bird that drops in the water. Duke knew very well what his soul's desire was: to get out in the ocean and swim around in the waves for hours.

However, Duke developed an annoying habit. After Christina would leave for work he'd hurriedly dig his way under the backyard fence, wriggle through, then race down to the beach five blocks away. Without pausing for breath, he'd zoom down the sand, launch himself into the Pacific Ocean and swim way out past all the surfers, then bodysurf his way back in to shore again.

That's why he was called Duke, after the legendary Hawaiian surfer.

The only trouble with this sport was that there was always a lifeguard waiting for him on the beach who'd clip a leash on him and bring him up to the clubhouse to be impounded by the dog ranger.

Well, Duke became a local celebrity and soon the locals were trying their best to help Christina avoid paying any more fines. They knew her work number from the disc on Duke's collar. Christina was an accountant who worked for a medium-sized accountancy firm nearby. If she had to go and fetch Duke from a good Samaritan down the street, she'd apologise to her boss, and treat the time as her lunch hour.

One day she was at work and received yet another phone call. Apparently a young surfer had caught Duke and was waiting in the car park.

When she arrived at the car park she thanked the young surfer then sighed as she fondled her dog's ears. 'Oh boy — what am I going to do with you, dopey dog? I can't keep leaving my job to pick you up. I'm not a taxi service, you know.'

The surfer laughed. 'Ah well. You can't really blame him, can you? He just loves to swim. Bit like me and my surfing.' He looked at Christina. 'Isn't there something you'd rather be doing right now instead of heading back to the office?'

'Of course there is but I guess I just think of my mortgage and bills and just grin and bear it,' she said. 'Doesn't everyone?'

The surfer gave the dog an admiring goodbye pat. 'Not me and Duke,' he said. 'We follow our soul first. Nothing gets between us and our surfing — not fences, rangers, bills or bosses.' With another grin he picked up his surfboard and started jogging down the sand to the water.

Beside her, Duke stared after the surfer and out at the waves and whined deep in his throat, trembling with eagerness to join his fellow surfer.

'Sorry — but no,' said Christina firmly. But as she reversed the car out of the car park, she cast one last look at the beautiful, glittering ocean. What do you really want to be doing right now? A voice in her mind asked. Because it sure as hell isn't driving back to that boring job of yours.

She braked suddenly, shocked at the unexpected thought. Was her job boring? Did she enjoy even being an accountant?

A horn honked in irritation behind her and she hurriedly drove off.

Crazy thoughts chased themselves around her head. She couldn't afford to have these thoughts, she decided in despair. She had a mortgage. The economic climate was dire. She had a safe, secure, respectable job.

'Too bad — I simply don't want to go back there,' she said out loud, astonished at how deeply she felt about it. 'I don't want to be an accountant anymore.'

She patted Duke, sitting on the passenger seat beside her — and thought of his overwhelming passion in life to swim.

'So what *would* you rather be doing?' she asked herself. 'If you could pick anything in the world — what would you rather be doing right this minute?'

The thought came to her immediately: Baking a magnificent cake.

She felt a smile curve her lips. Her grandmother and her mother had both been incredibly gifted cake makers and they'd taught her everything they knew. She laughed. She hadn't thought of baking a cake for years — and suddenly she felt a crazy urge to go home right now and make a beautiful, delicious cake.

She suddenly knew what she wanted to do with her life.

'I want to make fantastic cakes for other people to take pleasure in,' she said in excitement. 'Cakes that make special events truly unforgettable. Wedding cakes. Birthday cakes. Anniversary cakes. Celebrating the birth of a baby. Celebrating a milestone in someone's career. Important dinner party cakes. Cakes for expensive gourmet restaurants and upmarket cafes.'

Suddenly, her hands itched to get hold of some ingredients and her kitchen utensils — things she hadn't touched for years.

An unexpected thought blossomed in her mind: I've finally found what my soul desires. It felt wonderful, like all the pieces of her had finally come together to join in a smooth, tranquil whole.

'Come on, Duke, I've got to make a lot of changes when I get home,' she said, trembling with excitement.

If you're feeling a deep emptiness somewhere in your life then you haven't yet found what your soul desires. What can you do? Simply keep stopping throughout the day to pause and ask yourself, 'Is this really what I want to be doing right now?'

If you take the time your soul's desire will make itself felt.

7

What can dogs teach us about following our dreams?

Do you know where I've planned almost all my strategies for following my dreams? Out on my daily dog walks — especially those walks that take me far from the intrusions of other people and their problems. I don't think there's a better time to relax your mind, body and spirit than out on a relaxing dog walk. It's also a great place to get all three of these things working smoothly together so you can come up with your best and most creative ideas.

With my dogs at my side and Mother Nature all around, I'll tramp along tirelessly until the day's problems have fallen away and left my mind free to roam over all my ideas and options. Over days and weeks, each walk helps to filter my scattered thoughts until they eventually settle into a good, fluid strategy to tackle my dream.

I also believe dogs play an important support role when we follow our dreams — because they're with us every step of the way, aren't they? They sense when we're excited and love to be part of that wonderful energy when we reach our next milestone. They also sense when we're feeling deflated by an unforeseen obstacle and they comfort us with a lick and a loving look.

Quite simply, when everyone around us thinks we're crazy chasing our impossible dreams, our dog always gives us the feeling that we're never alone. Sometimes that can be the difference that makes our journey feel rich and exciting rather than scary and lonely. With a dog at my side, I always feel eager and ready to follow my dreams.

You're not really living your dream if you're just thinking about it

Stop thinking about your dream and start moving it along as soon as possible! Thinking about dreams endlessly is the easy part; you have to get out in the rough and tumble of making it happen. This is why I love watching dogs play-wrestle with each other. They're not just playing for the sake of it, they're actively chasing after their dream of perhaps one day becoming a top dog — the leader.

Becoming the leader of the pack is the ultimate dream for almost all dogs, no matter how tough or wimpy, big or small they are. It's the whole reason behind that constant play among dogs. Play-fighting is the instinctive way dogs gain the necessary experience to challenge their way up to the highly desirable and privileged leadership job.

They learn all the clever tricks and ingenious ploys of different dogs as well as learning all their own weaknesses and strengths. They build up their muscles and test their determination. They learn to take pain. They learn how to bluff their opponents. In other words, they learn over the years of playing with other dogs — or with humans — all the tricks of the trade of a top dog.

I can't help thinking that this process of play-fighting in the Dog World is a great lesson for anyone who knows what their dream is and yet hasn't progressed beyond thinking about it. Let's face it, as every dog knows, you need to plunge straight into the fray if you want to make your dream a reality.

One man who would not take that plunge was David. His dream was to write novels, however, all he did was read other people's published novels, and dream. Twelve years after I heard him say he wanted to write a novel, he was still dreaming.

'I've got the perfect story coming along,' he kept saying if anyone politely asked how his novel writing was progressing. 'It's all up here.' And he'd tap his head.

'When are you going to write it?' I asked.

'When it's perfect in my mind,' he said. 'It's not quite there yet, but don't worry — I'll know when it's ready.'

Eight years later, I ran into David again. I asked him how his novel writing was going.

'Brilliantly,' he said. 'I really do mean *brilliantly*, Martin.'

'Oh?'

'Yes, I've done a very good writing course since I last saw you,' he said. 'I've joined two different writers' groups. I now subscribe to an international writers' magazine and I volunteer to help at our local writers' centre. Oh — and I'm also going to a wonderful writers' festival later this year.'

'But any luck getting your great story down on paper yet?' I asked. David had once outlined his novel idea for me and I'd thought it sounded fantastic. His dream certainly wasn't empty — he had a great idea — but now he was long overdue at plunging in and getting his dream novel down on paper.

'My novel isn't quite perfect in my mind yet,' he said in a rather formal tone of voice. It was a polite warning that I was to stop asking uncomfortable questions.

I looked at him thoughtfully. I should veer away from the sensitive subject, that would be the polite thing to do. Unfortunately, when it comes to encouraging people to pursue their dreams, I feel too passionately to remain nicely polite.

'Right,' I said. I grabbed his arm and dragged him out of the café we were sitting in. I pulled him across to the big public park next door.

'What the hell?' spluttered David.

I didn't stop until we reached two teenage dogs I'd seen play-fighting through the café window. Both were really getting into it, making lots of bluff noise and thinking up some really fancy fight moves — but they were still only playing. There was no danger of this play-fight developing into a real fight.

'See that goofy dog there?' I said, pointing. 'Yeah, the dog that's making the most noise. Well at the moment you're not even making that much effort to get your novel written.'

'Gee, thanks, Martin. You're being real supportive,' he muttered.

'I *am* trying to support you,' I said in frustration. 'But I'm not mollycoddling you like you want me to do. Instead

I'm trying to give you a tough, necessary nudge to get that damn novel of yours written.'

He gave me a sulky look.

'You haven't even reached the hard part yet, David. You've got to get a publisher to pick your novel — and from what I know about the industry, that's going to be hellishly hard.'

'If the novel is good enough, it'll come to their attention. That's why I want it to be absolutely perfect in my mind before I write it,' he said.

'Look at those two dogs,' I said, 'and be inspired to plunge yourself into writing that fantastic novel of yours before you die of old age. Since puppyhood those two dogs have thrown themselves into the fray, desperately honing their play-fighting skills as often as they could.'

He flicked an uninterested look at the dogs still noisily play-wrestling.

'Now it's your turn,' I said. 'You need to get your novel down on paper and start the long process of pitching for an agent or a publisher, using every trick and skill you can think of.'

David looked mutinous. 'But —'

'No more buts. See for yourself — these dogs learn by doing. Otherwise they'd just be looking at each other, dreaming of how they'll one day develop the perfect fighting hold so they'll be a champion fighter without ever having to practice. So just start doing and learning. Write that damn novel!'

That was two years ago — and David still hasn't written his novel.

If you're pursuing your dream it doesn't really matter if people are laughing at you

One of the greatest freedoms in my life these days is simply not caring what everyone else thinks of me — especially when it comes to pursuing my dreams. However, it really helps your energy levels if you can learn to deal with all the naysayers who laugh when you mention what you hope to be doing some day. In my experience, the people who laugh the loudest are usually the ones who are the most envious. One of the best remedies for dealing with people like this is to take your dog for as many walks as you can — and simply get away from everyone.

Walking gets you breathing lots of mood-lightening oxygen. Take your dog for a great run along a deserted beach or river bank to shrug off all the negative, mocking comments. Or go for a wonderful moonlit night walk and look up at the stars and realise that the people who waste time mocking your goals are very small indeed in the universal scheme of things. Walk with your dog to a truly magnificent vista and sit and drink in the visual feast of Mother Nature in all her glory.

These were the kinds of walks I took with my own dogs over the years when my dreams weren't going to plan. When the pressures of my mortgage forced me to take a short-term job as a traffic controller — or lollipop man — I really attracted a lot of laughing. How my detractors had the time of their lives laughing at me! My pride took a big battering too, with all the quiet smirks on the job sites. As part of the training course we had to watch a health and safety training video. The actor who played the traffic controller in the training video went on to become one of Hollywood's biggest stars — Russell Crowe. Thinking of Russell Crowe certainly helped as I struggled to cope with the physically demanding job — standing in the freezing rain or the boiling sun for hours at a time. The job was pure torture for me because of my ADHD. Standing still on one spot for so many hours nearly drove me crazy. However, that job challenge passed as my career took off again and I left the mocking laughs and quiet smirks behind yet again.

So my lollipop man experience taught me that when your detractors get a chance to laugh at you, don't let them drag you down. Instead, switch them off as much as you can and take your faithful dog out for plenty of re-energising walks as far away from other people as you can get. Walking your dog gives you the chance to remind yourself exactly who you are and where you want to go. Let your generous-spirited dog remind you of why your dreams are so important to you.

Whatever you do, don't let small minds convince you that your dreams are too big. They aren't.

Stop mulling over your past mistakes and regrets

If you find you're still waiting for your dreams to begin and you just seem to be stuck in the same old rut, consider whether you're being held back by a tendency to dwell on your past mistakes and regrets. Staying stuck in the negative parts of your past is simply not going to put you in the right headspace you need to kick-start your dreams.

Mark wouldn't let go of his past so his dreams could unfold, even though his dog was such an inspiration to him as to how to embrace a much better future.

I knew Mark when I lived in the city: he was a brickie and I was a brickie's labourer. We used to sit around after working hard on the big city building sites all day, dreaming of how we'd like to one day live out in the country and have our own farms. Both of us missed being able to have a dog, as our small rented flats made that impossible. We'd sometimes sit on our apartment balconies deep in suburbia and stare up at the stars and discuss our dreams.

'One day you're going to move up north to your little farm,' Mark would say as he strummed beautiful, complicated pieces of music on his guitar. 'And you'll be able to have a pack of dogs living with you. I know that's when you'll somehow get all your crazy ideas about dogs published. Then you'll start working your butt off to make yourself into that great artist and poet you're always saying you can be.'

I'd hold up my mug of tea and toast that lovely, crazy vision.

'And you,' I said grandiosely, 'will move up north to your farm and become a much sought-after session musician with your own private recording studio. You'll compose music that famous bands will pay through the nose for.'

We'd clink tea mugs and raise them in salute to the stars.

The next day, of course, we'd both be off on the early train into the city to work.

Then came a day when I realised just how much time I wasted every day regurgitating my past mistakes and regrets.

It was clearly holding me back. I made a choice to get this big, dark cloud out of my life once and for all. So I did. The moment I dumped my mistakes and regrets, I immediately felt so much lighter.

Funny thing — as soon as you're not anchored down with all that dark, negative stuff you naturally start getting excited about your future.

Mark, however, couldn't seem to throw off his past — and our lives inevitably started growing apart.

The first thing I did when I finally moved north to a country village was get a rescue dog. As I took Fianna for her first walk down a beautiful country lane, I looked in wonder at all the clean space around me and thought, My God — I've actually done it! This is it — I've started living my dream.

Over the years, I kept making slow steps towards my next goal of getting my book on dogs published — and then slid backwards quite a way. It was a matter of staying determined and focused on grabbing any opportunities that came my way.

Meanwhile, Mark rang up occasionally from the city. 'How's it going up there?' he'd ask wistfully. 'I sure wish I could just take off and join you.'

'Do it,' I'd urge him. 'You can stay at my place until you get your feet under you. There's work up here if you look for it.'

But he wouldn't take the leap.

Gradually his phone calls became depressing, bitter things. All the mistakes and regrets he'd ever had were being replayed over and over like a broken record. He bought himself a beautiful dog called Sheba, a big, long-legged mongrel.

'Sheba would love living in the country — she hates being stuck in the city,' he kept moaning.

But I couldn't get him to venture north or pursue his dream any more. Mark always seemed to be stuck on the same page, doing exactly the same things, and still mulling over old regrets. Meanwhile, I was just getting on with things — trying to slog away at my dream step by step, until finally I got my first book on dogs published — and it became a bestseller.

Mark rang up after he saw me being interviewed on TV about my book being published despite not being able to read or write at the time. His voice was unusually subdued. 'Gee, Marty — you really made it happen, didn't you? You're on your way to living your dream life.'

'Come on,' I said. 'Come up north. Bring Sheba. It's time to kick-start that fantastic dream of yours — you're such a gifted musician.'

He was silent a moment. 'I can't,' he said. 'I found Sheba a new home. She hated being stuck in the city.

'Marty, I don't think I have the energy to believe in dreams any more. I should have gone north when I was younger. I had my chance to go north and I blew it. I can't believe I sold my guitar. I wish I hadn't given away my great dog ... '

I haven't bothered ringing Mark for a while now. These days I don't even have the energy to deal with someone else's old mistakes and past regrets — I'm just too busy working towards my own dreams.

It's wake-up time for all dreamers out there! If you're curious to see whether the dream can unfold into reality then get into the right headspace. You need to be so full of energy, strength and determination to kick-start yourself into action. Your head needs to be focusing full time on creative problem-solving as each obstacle looms up at you.

If you decide to genuinely chase your dreams then you're about to begin the greatest adventure of your life — and your mind can only deal with the exciting future. So get rid of all your past mistakes and regrets. You simply haven't got enough space inside your mind to think about them any more.

Lose the paralysing fear of pursuing your dream

The best way to lose that horrible fear of chasing your dream is to simply start doing something about it — and I don't mean thinking. Follow your heart and do some big or small action that will keep moving your dream along.

Laurie finally got the courage to do something about his dream career when he watched his dog swimming in the park pond.

I met Laurie at a big dog-walking park — we fell into conversation while watching the dogs playing in the park's big pond. I was watching the beautiful, charming King Charles Spaniel called Lady I was babysitting while Laurie watched his Kelpie-cross-Labrador, Mulligan.

'Look at what a wimp Lady is,' I said, laughing. She was sitting delicately right on the edge of the pond with a nervous expression on her face, desperate to join the other dogs for a swim but too scared to get so much as a toe wet.

'Bit different from your dog. Look at what a crazy madcap creature he is.'

Mulligan was having the time of his life: running at full speed around the pond, then taking a leaping jump off a big log. He'd land far out into the pond with a huge splash.

'Yes,' Laurie said, 'he's a real dare devil.' He watched his dog for a moment. 'Hell — I wish I had a fraction of his courage.'

'Why? What do you mean?'

'I'm so frustrated with my own cowardice these days,' he admitted. 'I'm stuck in a civil service job I no longer enjoy. What I really wanted to do when I was a young man was to become a furniture designer.' He laughed in a self-deprecating way. 'I actually showed quite a flair for it.'

'Why didn't you follow it up when you were younger?' I asked.

'Usual reasons. Unenthusiastic reaction from my parents. Teachers being negative about it as a career. The paralysing fear of failing and being left with no career prospects. But now I'm fifty,' he said. 'I can't help feeling that I should give it one last shot. You know — a matter of now or never.'

'Good on you. That's very brave.'

'Oh no — I'm not giving up my job, not this close to getting my pension. I'm not crazy. I just want to see if I can design some beautiful furniture in my spare time.'

'Well? What's stopping you? That sounds pretty safe and sensible.'

He looked back at the madcap antics of Mulligan, who was thoroughly enjoying himself in the water, making as much noise and splashing as he could.

'I have to admit I'm scared of starting because I'm scared of failing. I'm paralysed by fear, scared that I might prove to myself once and for all that I *can't* design furniture — that I have absolutely no talent for it. Otherwise, what will I have left then?'

'Huh?'

'I'll have no secret dream to keep at the back of my mind. I'm really terrified of finally testing my talent.'

I said nothing but watched Mulligan as he plunged with no fear, no hesitation, into the water — and he did it with such pride and pure wild happiness.

'I think your best inspiration is Mulligan,' I said. 'Whenever you need to gain courage just bring him here and let him jump in the water. Remind yourself about letting go of all your doubts and fears — and just leap right in.'

'I'll never have his courage when it comes to chasing my dream.'

He was to prove himself wrong.

I ran into Laurie four years later at an art gallery and he was like a different man. He stood taller and carried an aura of confidence. I hardly recognised him.

He walked up and gave me a big hug.

'You'll be happy to hear I've started chasing my dream,' Laurie said proudly. 'I can hardly believe it myself. Of course I would never have got the courage together except for Mulligan. You were right — he's a great inspiration if I ever have doubts about myself.'

He explained he'd started tinkering away on some secret furniture designs in his garage on the weekend and he'd spent his evenings after work researching contemporary furniture design on the internet.

'But my real turning point,' he said, 'was when I went to a big international design fair and was very *un*inspired. I actually looked around at a lot of the pieces on exhibition and thought, Hey — surely I can do better than this junk.'

That was the trigger, he explained, that really kick-started him into becoming serious about furniture design.

'I think that's when I started going a bit Mulligan. You know — just leaping out and plunging straight in. Being fearless and happily so. I guess that's when my work started moving up to a whole new level.'

He looked at me proudly. 'Lately, I've started getting some very exciting commissions — hotels, private collectors. To be honest, I don't care if I never make a living out of it, I'm just so excited that I finally proved to myself that I have a talent for design. Now when I flick through a design magazine, I don't have that vague angry and frustrated feeling deep inside my gut. I feel like I'm a part of the industry now. I'm no longer an outsider looking hopefully in, wishing I belonged. I belong now. I'm chasing my dream.'

If you have a dream, lose that paralysing fear however you can and just start taking action. Start small, make mistakes, get inspired, get involved, get better — just follow your dream. Believe me, if some former street kid like me can do it, so can you. I bet once you start, you'll be kicking yourself for not taking up your dream years earlier!

How do I want the world to be different because I lived in it?

Have you ever wondered how you could make the world a better place because you live in it?

I have. My big dream is that one day humans all over the world will learn to communicate better with dogs by learning the International Language of Dogs — and I want to help that happen. However, I have a small dream too. Everywhere I go, I like helping people communicate a little bit better with each other. I want to make the world different in a really big way but also in a small way. What ideas do you have?

Allie and I occasionally walked our dogs together when I lived in a small country village. Her dog, Roger, was a brindle French Bulldog. If you're unfamiliar with this breed they're comical characters with a funny little snub-nosed, gargoyle face with small bat ears and a sturdy body. Roger was an affectionate fellow and got on really well with my own pack of rescue hounds. Allie and Roger didn't cross my path often because while I liked walking my hounds down the railway line, she preferred walking her dog on the outskirts of the village.

One day I decided to join them on their favourite walk. We got to the stretch of public land — perhaps twenty acres in size — and Allie released Roger for a gallop.

'Gee, it's not a very inspiring place to walk, is it?' Allie said. 'No trees, no wildlife — just a barbed wire fence stretched around a big rectangle of roughly mown grass.'

'That's why I prefer the railway line,' I said. 'There are so many birds and animals living in the long grass and bushes along the way. It's actually a very private and tranquil place.'

Allie looked around in distaste. 'God knows why I bother walking here at all.'

'So change it,' I said.

'What?'

'Why don't you do something about it? You know, make it into a place you'll really love visiting every day with Roger.'

She looked at me then laughed. 'Martin, you make it sound so simple.' She rubbed her head. 'I've got a headache just thinking of all the rules and red-tape involved.'

'Yep — that's probably why no one's bothered to do anything about it up until now. But take it a step at a time and see it happen.'

Amazingly, Allie did set about fixing up that park and making it a sanctuary for the local wildlife while keeping it a place suitable for walking dogs. In the end, her project took three years to complete to the first stage — and by then it was a truly beautiful place. Now instead of twenty acres of rough grass, there are long gallop areas of smoothly mown grass and other more intimate winding pathways. There are hundreds of native trees and shrubs and a fenced-in area where people can let their dogs run free without fear of them running out on to the road nearby.

Allie gave me a grand tour the day before its official opening.

'Here's the project that's turned into my own personal baby,' she said. She stood proudly before a long line of sturdy cage fencing. Inside was crammed with thorny, spiny, sharp plants of all sizes.

'Um — that's nice.' Some people like pretty rose gardens, I guessed. Maybe other people like gardens full of sharp, ugly plants.

She caught sight of my face and laughed. 'It's not a flower garden, Martin. Look at what it's full of beside sharp thorns. Look closer!'

I looked at the garden and then I realised what she meant.

'Wow, Allie — that's incredible,' I said and gave her a big hug of congratulation.

The garden was absolutely packed with shifting clouds of tiny wrens and other native birds.

'It's a wren garden,' she said. 'When I was researching native gardens I read that wrens and other small native birds are at risk of getting killed by cats and their native habitat is being destroyed. All they need is plenty of prickly, thorny bushes planted together and they start moving in and nesting.

'I love this whole park — they're even thinking of naming it after me. But —' She gestured at her wren garden. 'This will be the thing I'm most proud of in my life. Just imagine how many generations of tiny little birds will live here? How many wren generations will end up breeding here? Why just imagine if this garden is still here in a hundred years? I'm thrilled with it.'

I hugged her again. 'Well done, darling. It's a fantastic project.'

Looking at her, I knew her life would always taste especially good knowing she'd made this small, but amazing difference to the world.

Allie and Roger loved walking in the wildlife sanctuary they'd helped to create out of a bare grass paddock.

Only you can decide how to live a life that makes you proud. Make choices so that at the end of your life you can look back and know your life mattered. Live a life filled with purpose. Think of both big ways and small ways you can change the world for the better. To my way of thinking, this is how we all help to build a civilisation we can be proud of. With or without your dog at your side — make a difference to the world.

Epilogue

Are you ready to see your dog as your teacher yet?

We've now reached the end of this book's journey and I hope I've shown you how your dog can turn out to be an influential teacher in your life. We've met dogs who taught their humans about happiness and more about themselves. We've met dogs who taught their owners how to creatively solve problems and advance their careers. We've met dogs who showed their owners different ways they could improve their relationships. And we've also met dogs who taught their humans how to bring more spirituality into their lives, as well as how to pursue their dreams fearlessly as well as more strategically. There's no denying that dogs transform human lives.

Look at me — I'm a living example of how dogs can help you become a better person. Over the years, dogs have turned my life inside out and upside down and shaken me until I had to stop messing around and simply grow up. Today I'm deeply proud of the man I've grown into, and believe me, when I was a young, freakish, skinny kid in Garryowen, I *never* thought I'd be able to say that about myself!

So from now on keep an eye on what your dog is trying to teach you about yourself because I believe every single dog out there has something to teach us about how to live a better, happier and wiser life.

If you were wondering how I helped the owners in this book solve their dog behaviour problems, you can learn my techniques from my book *What's Your Dog Telling You?* If you haven't read it yet, I highly recommend you pick up a copy. Most dog problems are actually very easy to sort out — but only once you learn what your dog is *really* trying to tell you.

That's why *What's Your Dog Telling You?* is so different to other dog books — it shows you how to become incredibly fluent in the International Language of Dogs. By the last page you'll be able to fix almost any behaviour problem — as well as hold a genuine conversation with every dog you meet! How many dog books can teach you how to do that?

Acknowledgments

I'd like to thank the fantastic humans in my pack: Lee, Siggy, Casey, Fintan and Marie — I love you all so dearly.

As well, I'd like to thank my own dogs. Life's never boring with you lot around to keep me on my toes.

I'd also like to thank the really impressive lead dogs I've known over the years: you've all taught me basically everything I know — especially you, Jack.

Thanks, too, to my very supportive triplet brothers, John and Andrew and, of course, to Mammy, who was a very special woman.

WHAT'S YOUR DOG TELLING YOU

?

Australia's best-known dog communicator on how to
UNDERSTAND and **IMPROVE** your dog's behaviour

Martin McKenna

Bestselling author of *The Dog Man*